HUNT FOR GOLD

HUNT FOR GOLD

SUNKEN GALLEONS IN THE NEW WORLD

JOHN CHRISTOPHER FINE

Palm Beach Florida

An imprint of Globe Pequot, the trade division of
The Rowman & Littlefield Publishing Group, Inc.
4501 Forbes Blvd., Ste. 200
Lanham, MD 20706
www.rowman.com

Distributed by NATIONAL BOOK NETWORK

British Library Cataloguing in Publication Information available

Library of Congress Cataloging-in-Publication Data available

Names: Fine, John Christopher, author.
Title: Hunt for gold : sunken galleons in the New World / John Christopher Fine.
Description: Palm Beach, Florida : Pineapple Press, 2022. | Includes index.
Identifiers: LCCN 2022003253 (print) | LCCN 2022003254 (ebook) | ISBN 9781683343219 (cloth) | ISBN 9781683343226 (ebook)
Subjects: LCSH: Weller, Robert. | Weller, Margaret Ann. | Shipwrecks—Florida. | Scuba divers—Florida—Biography.
Classification: LCC CT9971.W45 F56 2022 (print) | LCC CT9971.W45 (ebook) | DDC 917.5904—dc23/eng/20220308
LC record available at https://lccn.loc.gov/2022003253
LC ebook record available at https://lccn.loc.gov/2022003254

™ The paper used in this publication meets the minimum requirements of American National Standard for Information Sciences—Permanence of Paper for Printed Library Materials, ANSI/NISO Z39.48-1992.

CONTENTS

Taffi Fisher Abt, Bob "Frogfoot" Weller, and Margaret Weller, with the Queen's Jewels.

Gold jewels studded with diamonds dubbed "The Queen's Jewels" with a golden earwax remover and toothpick.

Left: Bob and Margaret Weller documenting treasure coins found on a Spanish galleon on film.

FOREWORD

JOHN CHRISTOPHER FINE IS A STORY BY HIMSELF AND I HOPE that someday he will undertake an autobiography. In the meantime, he has undertaken quite a task in this biography of Bob and Margaret Weller. Both of the Wellers should be considered explorers and pioneers in the field of underwater treasure hunting, along with my parents, Mel and Dolores "Deo" Fisher. They share the same spirit and determination needed to succeed in this field. Much like my dad, Bob Weller has always been enthusiastic and optimistic (with Margaret constantly working and helping at his side) in a field where governments seek to control, piracy lurks, and only if you are very persistent, dreams unfold into fantastic realities!

In addition to being treasure finders, I have always admired the way Bob and Margaret strive to share their stories and knowledge with others. This has been accomplished through publishing many of their own books about shipwreck salvage. They have also done countless exhibitions and lectures and in the last decade, they developed an "Introduction Course to Shipwreck Archaeology and Salvage." The program they have established is quite popular and informative. It gives newcomers into the field a hands-on learning experience which could not be duplicated in any University classroom. I believe it is their way of giving back to the world, encouraging the upcoming generations to continue to explore, look for adventure, and follow their dreams.

The author, John Christopher Fine.

I vividly remember the day Bob called on the VHF radio, trying to keep his voice calm. "Taffi, you may want to meet us at the dock with a couple of reporters." When Bob pulled his boat, the *Pandion*, up to the dock, he could barely contain his excitement. The whole crew had the most radiant smiles on their faces. Newspaper photographers and writers pushed and shoved to see what it was all about.

"Come aboard Taffi, I have something to show you. . . ." He said as he held out his hand to help me aboard. When they slowly and delicately unwrapped the towel on the engine cover, there it was, a brilliant, dazzling, blindingly beautiful four-piece diamond jewelry set. The treasures glistened in the sunlight. The set, including two large (about the size of the palm of your hand) unique brooches, one shaped like a butterfly and one shaped like a flower and a matched set of earrings, contained a total of 427 sparkling rare gray diamonds. The flashbulbs flashed, but not as big as the smiles on Bob and Margaret's faces.

Some days, we treasure hunters may consider it drudgery. Day after day navigating, searching thousands of miles of ocean, constantly struggling for funding. As most of you know, a boat is a bottomless money pit. The trials are many in this business, the unending searching, the majority of the time not finding. Boats and equipment break down. There are shark encounters, weathering frightening storms at sea that just sneak up on you. And of course, the ever constant danger of boating and diving accidents involved in such a high-risk occupation which sometimes results in extreme and personal tragedies.

Yet, when you persevere, one day, you can say, as my dad, Mel Fisher, and Bob and Margaret have, "Today's the Day!" You find some fantastic treasure that most people have only dreamt or read about. A piece of history! You become a part of it, consumed by it. It's a powerful ocean, full of stories, danger, history, fun, romance, and adventure. Enjoy diving into it with John Christopher Fine and the Wellers.

—Taffi Fisher Abt
President of Mel Fisher Center Incorporated,
operators of Mel Fisher Treasure Museum in Sebastian, Florida
and Vice President of Mel Fisher Enterprises

INTRODUCTION

"I WAS DOWN SIXTEEN-FEET. VISIBILITY WAS SEVENTY-FIVE, a hundred-foot. The water was warm." Robert Weller sat in a deep, soft leather chair in the living room of his home in Florida. Fire crackled in a brick hearth warming the room. It was winter. The treasure diving season in Florida was over for the year.

"The wind was starting to pick up. Underwater there was flat sand scattered with coral in small mounds," Weller picked up the story. He spoke casually, his hands and blue eyes animated. He could visualize the moment as he described what happened.

"The boat suddenly started to move. What was happening above was one of our boat lines tangled with another boat working nearby. It was wrapped around John Brandon's stern line. I was still below. Margaret and Bob Luyendyk had to let out about seventy-five feet of line so Mike Maguire, one of the divers on Brandon's crew, could get their anchor up. Maguire swam over to untangle his anchor."

"Meantime I'm on the bottom and, because the wind had picked up, I'm bouncing along down there at a pretty good pace." Robert "Bob" Weller, called Frogfoot since his Navy days, had a regulator in his mouth attached to a long air hose hooked to a compressor aboard the boat. He was being dragged along the bottom by the regulator hose.

"They finally got the crossed lines loose and took a turn on the bow line. I found myself in a new place. Topside Bob Luyendyk and my wife Margaret tried to pull us back to where we were. The wind was too strong; they couldn't pull against it. The conversation aboard went something like, 'We haven't dug a hole here before. See if Bob wants us to dig a hole.' They gave me two pulls on the line. I gave them two pulls back that said go ahead," Weller smiled.

The *Pandion*, Weller's treasure hunting boat, was equipped with a blower. It is an elbow-like device that can be lowered down over the ship's propeller. The blower directs the boat's prop wash downward over the site.

Bob Weller leans over the stern of *Pandion* giving a diver instructions.

Divers work below in the prop wash as the cover of sand is blown away to search for artifacts. As long as the boat is properly anchored, it does not move until the crew uses winches to pull in on stout anchor lines that are paid out, one forward and two sideways off the stern.

"They fired up the engine and started digging. The sand was almost two feet deep there. Lots of curious fish. I could vaguely see a reef shoreward from me about fifty feet away. There was nothing in that hole."

"Margaret gave me two tugs on the air hose. Do I want to move? Two tugs back. Go ahead. They moved the boat about three feet and started blowing another hole. It was a new area we hadn't worked before."

The story took time. Like most of Weller's tales of high adventure underwater, the telling built after a listener's imagination was piqued.

"Suddenly there was this pottery shard from an olive jar. I picked it up and said, 'Man this is nice.' I held the pottery shard in one hand, my metal detector in the other." He didn't let more go until the story built up suspense; he knew he had the listener hooked.

Oil painting in the Weller collection depicting storm-tossed galleons.

"The conversation up on the boat was, 'It's getting close to five o'clock. Let's blow one more hole and go home.' They moved the boat three feet and blew the third hole."

"In the middle of that third hole was a bundle of a gold chain. It was all in a bundle." Weller balled up his cupped hands.

"I knew what it was. I just didn't know how long it was. My heart beat pretty fast about that time. I gathered up the gold chain in one hand, swung the metal detector around the outside of the hole to make sure nothing else was there and headed for the surface."

"Up on the boat Margaret and Bob Luyendyk were in the cabin near the console. They heard a grunting. Margaret said to Bob Luyendyk, 'What's that?' Bob said, 'Probably the radio.' Margaret said, 'No I think that's Bob.' Margaret walked to the back of the boat." Weller laughed as he recalled the incident.

"Here I am in the water. Metal detector in one hand. Pottery shard and gold chain in the other. Nothing to grab the boarding ladder with. If I spit out the regulator to shout there's no hand left to put it back with.

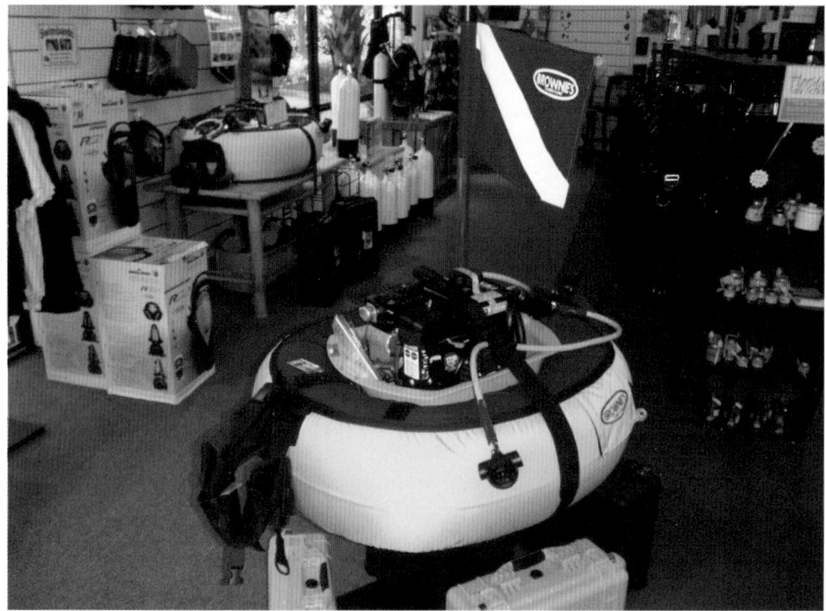

Divers like the Wellers and many others use unique tools and devices to assist on their explorations. This is a hookah rig. A gasoline engine powers a compressor that feeds air into a long hose attached to a dive regulator.

With my weight belt I'd slip back under. The waves now are about three feet high."

"I held up the pottery shard and gold chain, handed them up to Margaret so I could grab the boarding ladder. I got the regulator mouthpiece out and said, 'That's got to be at least three feet long.'"

"Margaret had marked the deck in increments of one foot so when we let out line on the anchors, we'd know how much we let out. When she stretched the gold chain out on the floorboards it was over nine feet, the limit of her marks along the deck." The long gold chain was the best artifact found that year from sunken remnants of the 1715 Spanish plate fleet that broke up and came ashore along Florida's coast between Fort Pierce and Sebastian.

The gold chain measured eleven feet two inches in length. It was found on the *Nieves* wreck site about nine hundred feet off the beach opposite a place salvors' knew as B Marker.

The Weller team, Margaret is on the left flanked by Bob on the right as divers are about to roll backward off the dive boat to explore a site where the 1715 Spanish treasure fleet wrecked near Fort Pierce, Florida.

Bob and Margaret Weller aboard *Pandion* taking bearings during a long day diving on the 1715 fleet.

Diver John McSherry with a Tumbaga lump of silver he recovered in the Bahamas.

That afternoon, lanky, six-foot tall Bob "Frogfoot" Weller, of Irish ancestry, did a jig on the fantail.

This discovery, and other exploits by Bob and Margaret Weller, and their teams of divers, is the stuff dreams are made of.

Frogfoot is gone now. He "passed over the bar," as he was fond of saying when a pioneer diver died, in 2008. His friend and mentor, the legendary treasure diver Mel Fisher, died in 1998. Many continue in the pursuit of sunken treasure and have become legends in their own right.

Navy combat veteran John McSherry, a Top Gun fighter pilot in the Vietnam War, discovered rare silver bars in Bahamas' waters. McSherry is convinced that much of that sunken treasure remains yet unfound. He is embarking on a project to find it.

Share the adventures of sunken treasure tales as we join diving legends that have searched for and found the stuff dreams are made of.

1

DETROIT RIVER DAYS

ROBERT WELLER WAS BORN ON MAY 20, 1925, IN MONROE, Michigan. He grew up in Wyandotte where he lived with his family in a boathouse on the Detroit River.

"Dad was of Irish ancestry born in the U.S., there was some German in the Weller family. I traced our family tree back to the 1700s," Bob said. He put his hands behind his neck and smiled. This was a signal. A story was coming.

"Commodore David Porter was my Great Great Uncle. He chased the pirates off the Barbary Coast. My Great Grandmother was a Porter. Her husband's uncle was Commodore David Porter. My grandmother's name was Speer from the Vanwert, Ohio area. Grandpa was a farmer but moved to Michigan about the time I was born," Weller recounted.

FAMILY HISTORY

Weller's father was a professional photographer. He worked for Fox Movietone during the war. An athlete, he boxed and played tennis. His mother was always a housekeeper.

"We were pretty poor. We went through prohibition and the depression. It was a time when all you were doing was trying to make a living." Weller recalled his growing up.

"We had to put cardboard in our shoes to keep out snow. My older brother and I used to peddle papers. The *Detroit News*, *Times* and *Free Press*." Weller had one older brother. There was a three-year difference in their ages.

"In those days if you put a hundred advertisements for a local grocery store on door knobs they gave you twenty-five cents. That was 1932. I bought a pineapple pie for five cents, gave twenty cents to my mother," Weller said. It took a long time for the story of his youth to unfold. Each memory was savored as though he could picture every event.

For all of his military combat experience, Bob Weller remained the sentimental, good-natured man of his youth. Even up to his death on October 13, 2008, he remained an avid storyteller with recall for detail that could enthrall and put a listener into the action.

"We rented houses. My mother took in boarders. When my father divorced her, I was five. Jack Craven was one of the boarders. I didn't know it then but he was an escaped prisoner from a chain gang in Georgia. His real name was Douglas."

"Craven was a great father. They never caught him. He was a big fellow. I had a lot of respect for him." Reality changed the look in Bob's eyes. "I once called his sister in Clearwater, Florida to find out about him after he died. She hung up on me." Weller shook his head, dismayed.

"Jack used to take us fishing. He was more a father than my real father was."

Bob Weller was a swimming champion in college and in the U.S. Navy. U.S. NAVY, PHOTO COURTESY OF BOB WELLER

Weller developed his stamina swimming across the Detroit River dodging ore carriers. It gave him the competitive instincts he needed for sports.

"I swam all through high school. During those four years our high school team won every meet," he said. Weller swam freestyle and backstroke. Photographs from his high school days show a tall, six-foot, powerfully built athletic Bob Weller, confident and eager.

U.S. NAVY

"In May 1943, I was taking trigonometry and aerodynamics so I could get into college. I was going to school after my class graduated to take two more classes."

"My homeroom teacher told me they were giving an examination for the Navy V 12 program. 'Here's your chance to go to college,' the homeroom teacher told me. I went to the library and signed up. It was full of people taking the test that already started a half-hour before. I sat down, wrote the exam and was the first one finished," Weller said.

Weller passed the exam. Two weeks later he was notified by the Navy to go to Detroit and take a physical examination. He passed the rigorous physical tests and was signed up for the U.S. Navy V 12 program.

"They sent students to various colleges around the U.S. for four semesters. Along with the regular courses they gave you seamanship and navigation. I took my first train ride from Detroit to Williamstown, Massachusetts. There were no seats available so I stood up for the better part of a day," Weller said.

Weller carried twenty-four points that first semester at Williams College. Naval officer training was rigorous. "We went to class six days a week from 7 AM to 6 PM. Of the 480 of us that started some 200 graduated."

The gleam in Weller's eyes signaled another tale coming. "We had to keep a good average. We could get no more than fifty demerits a semester. I got fifty-five in one day," he smiled.

"I started swimming with the college swim team. We won all our meets. I became one of the New England Intercollegiate Swimming Champions." Weller began the tale of the Navy demerits that nearly ended his military career before it began. "I was coached by Bob Muir. Was on the Williams varsity swim team. We won all our meets that year and took the New England Intercollegiate Championships held at M.I.T." "I was on the first-place medley relay team. We did really well, we were good swimmers. We hitchhiked to the New York State Swimming Championships and brought home a bunch of medals. I was a strong swimmer. Living on the river in Detroit you have no choice. It was fun to dodge the freighters as I swam across. We went to Yale in 1944 for the Nationals, and we did very well for a small college."

The story was taking a detour. "Dick Lyons was captain of the Yale swim team. Charlie Gillette was on the backstroke. I swam against him. Fast forward," Weller said. The detour was taking another detour. "Those two were in my Navy UDT class in Coronado, California."

The demerits: "There was a notice on the bulletin board that everyone should eat in undress whites. We went to classes in dungarees. I sat eating my lunch in dungarees." "Bucky Walters the Commanding Officer said 'What's the meaning of this. I'll see you after muster.' At muster demerits were published. Apprentice Seaman Robert Weller, twenty-five demerits for failing to stand to attention in the presence of an officer. Twenty-five for failing to obey a posted order, five for eating out of uniform. I got fifty-five demerits in two minutes."

"There was a big announcement in the newspaper that we won the New England swimming championships." That gave Weller a second chance. Commander Walters told him that if he received a grade of C or better in all of his courses, he would send Weller to Midshipman's school and waive the demerits.

It wasn't easy. "I was getting an F in calculus and was doing poor in psychology. I really hit the books for the next ten days. I got a C in calculus and a C in psychology. It turned out the swim coach knew the psychology professor and told him the kid needed a break."

Bob Weller went to Midshipman's School at Fort Schuyler, New York from November 1944 until February 1945. He received his commission at ceremonies held at St. John's Cathedral in New York City.

Weller was sent to Navy Line Officers School in Miami for two-and-a-half months. "I learned to fly while there. I logged 7 hours 45 minutes in a seaplane with the instructor and did a fifteen-minute solo flight. I have the solo certificate in my sea chest."

Weller's first navy assignment was aboard the *Arequipa* an AF 31 refrigerator ship. "I caught up with it in Manila in the Philippines." Weller spent the rest of World War II traveling between the Philippines and Australia.

The *Arequipa* was caught in a typhoon when the war ended and it was heading back to the United States. "Waves were eighty-five feet high off Guam. The only two people not sick were the quartermaster on duty and me. I spent twenty-eight hours on watch without food or even a cup of coffee."

A sixteen inch "I" beam on *Arequipa*'s starboard side fractured. Only steel plates on the ship's side held it together. It chugged back to port disabled.

"Potentially we could sink at any time. Ships would pass us from one to the next reporting our position until we got to Long Beach. We pulled alongside the *Nevada*. It was painted orange. What a beacon. It was headed for the Bikini tests," Weller said.

Weller was transferred to the *George Clymer* PA 27. He was now a first lieutenant and headed up the boat division for amphibious landings. Weller was discharged from the Navy in December 1946.

BACK HOME AFTER THE WAR

"I had just gotten married to Pat in September 1946. I came back home to Michigan and got a job as a shift worker at Wyandotte Chemical Company. I was a laboratory technician. I started work at midnight so I could go to class at the University of Detroit during the day. I hitchhiked thirty miles into Detroit to go to class and hitchhiked back." Weller did not own a car.

The Wellers bought a brick home for $7,800. It was a two-bedroom, one-bath house with a basement that flooded during heavy rain.

Their first son was born in October 1947. He managed one full semester at the University of Detroit. "We couldn't afford any furniture in the house. It was mortgaged. We had one small table in the kitchen and two chairs. A bed and dresser in the bedroom and a blue sofa and mirror in the front room."

BACK IN THE NAVY

"One day I opened the hall closet. My Navy hat was on a shelf. I put it on. My first wife Pat looked and said, 'Now I know why I married you. You looked so good in uniform.' I asked her, whether she would like to see me back in uniform. 'Just fine,' Pat answered. 'This is a rat race,' she said."

"I wrote a letter to the Navy that night and said I wanted to go back on active duty. They wrote back to report for a physical examination. I passed

Bob Weller with his U.S. Navy Officers hat and automatic pistol with his medals at Weller's Cove.

it and reported for duty aboard the aircraft carrier *Antietam* in San Francisco in 1947."

When he reported for duty, he was embarrassed. "My World War II uniforms were threadbare. I only had khakis. I had no shoes. The Commander loaned me ten dollars to buy shoes. I bought brown shoes to match my uniform. It was embarrassing."

Bob didn't have enough money at first to bring his family out to San Francisco. Gradually the financial situation improved, and the family rented Navy housing in Alameda.

Hollywood chose the *Antietam* as a set for the movie *Task Force* starring Gary Cooper and Walter Brennan. "I had a speaking part in it," Bob said.

The 1949 motion picture *Task Force* stars Gary Cooper (left), Walter Brennan (middle), and Wayne Morris (right). U.S. NAVY, PHOTO COURTESY OF BOB WELLER.

After the movie was wrapped up, the Navy decommissioned *Antietam*. "I was in the deck division. Wolf Hainberg and I were the last officers aboard. They transferred me to the heavy cruiser *Helena* a CA 75. I was assigned to the First Lieutenant's department."

He got the assignment of athletic director and public information officer. The *Helena* had a four-destroyer escort. The ship was ordered to the Pacific. It was summer cruise training for ROTC upper classmen. Many were college athletes. The Navy decided to participate in the Pan Am games in Panama. Weller was put in charge of getting the contestants ready.

"Every morning at 6 AM I was in the eight-inch gun mount leading calisthenics. We got down to Balboa on Panama's Pacific side. We did pretty well in the Pan American games. I participated on the swim team," he said, producing a trophy he won in Panama.

BACK AGAIN TO CIVILIAN LIFE

Weller was to be discharged 1 July. They kept him on four more months until the Pan Am games were over. The Weller family moved back to Navy housing in Alameda, California. Bob attended the University of California at Berkley and finally earned a degree in Architectural Engineering.

"When I graduated from UC Berkley, I had no job. I was married and had two kids. I had been teaching aquatics at the Oakland YMCA. The Central YMCA in San Francisco had a summer camp in Santa Cruz, they offered me a job. They had the largest outdoor Olympic size pool in the State of California. I moved the family to a house they provided for us at the camp. We had a lot of fun that summer. It was a great place for our sons Bobby and Richard to grow up."

It was the summer the Korean War started. A chance meeting with one of the kid's parents at summer camp brought Weller back into the Navy.

"We put on shows. There was a boy's camp and a girl's camp. When the parents came out to pick up their kids we had aquatic skits. Synchronized swimming, clowns. I met one of the parents. A Lieutenant Commander in the Navy Chaplain Corps. He was sitting in the audience. We got to talking and I mentioned I had been in the Navy."

NEW ENLISTMENT

This chance encounter and the chaplain's comment that the Navy needed line officers gave Weller incentive to write the Navy indicating he was interested in returning to duty. "Within a week I got a telegram back giving me five days to report to Detroit for a physical."

Weller was ordered to report to the Light Cruiser *Manchester* CL 73. *Manchester* was already in the Korean Theater. He boarded a troop transport to Formosa. The *Manchester* arrived in Formosa the same day Weller got into port. Weller drank local water and came down with dysentery. His first two weeks were spent in sick bay. He was too ill to enjoy liberty ashore in Taiwan.

Weller was *Manchester*'s public information officer, helicopter gunfire spotter, gunnery main battery control officer and first division officer. "There were not many Navy officers aboard with World War II experience," he said.

PRELUDE TO KOREA

"I was in on the invasion of Sin Do and So Do Islands. We were in Wonsan Harbor in the middle of winter. It was cold. There was ice on the rigging, ice on the deck. It was the most inhospitable place you can be. We got shot at frequently."

"We had a V.I.P. come aboard. Phil Bucklew was one of the big heroes of World War II with Navy demolition teams. We became friends, used to play *Acey Deucy* in the wardroom. He told me the Navy was looking for good swimmers for Underwater Demolition Teams. I put in for it and was assigned to UDT training in Coronado, California when our ship got back to the U.S."

One of Weller's best Navy assignments came when he was flown home two weeks before the *Manchester* was due to make port in Long Beach, California. As public information officer he was tasked with the duty to set up a homecoming for the ship.

"I contacted a doctor; his name was Nolan. He catered to the stars. The doctor said he would be glad to help me. The next day the doctor had Dagwood Bumstead and his wife at his house. Dagwood and his neighbor 'Woody' said they'd be glad to help. There was a party at Hearst Castle and Hearst's mistress Marion Davies called and said you're invited." Weller smiled, this Navy duty was easy to take.

A DATE WITH MARILYN MONROE

The party included Dorothy Lamour and Barbara Hale. They said they'd help. "There was a studio dormitory for young actresses. The rule was no smoking, no drinking. The girls had to be in by 11 PM. I met Marilyn Monroe." Weller's smile broadened.

It was one of his contented smiles punctuated with a long pause while he closed his eyes, put his hands behind his head, and rocked back in the swivel chair in his office. He savored the memory.

Weller had *Manchester* construct a stage on the stern that could accommodate a piano. The big day came, and Weller introduced Allan Mobry who was the emcee.

"That morning Tommy Dorsey sent a telegram. Every officer was invited to hear him play on Saturday at the Hollywood Palladium."

Bob Weller at the homecoming of his ship. U.S. NAVY, PHOTO COURTESY OF BOB WELLER.

Movie stars would participate in homecoming of warships. Marilyn Monroe is seated in the middle behind star Monica Sellers. U.S. NAVY, PHOTO COURTESY OF BOB WELLER.

"The first girl to leave the homecoming early was Marilyn Monroe. They had just handed me Tommy Dorsey's telegram. I showed it to her and asked if she would like to go." If Weller's first smile was wide, he now grinned until his face resembled the image of a contented Cheshire cat.

"I still had the use of two limos that weekend. We picked the girls up and went to the Brown Derby for dinner and then the Palladium. Marilyn was very bright and very personable. She kissed me on the cheek. I didn't wash for a week," Weller laughed.

UNDERWATER DEMOLITION TRAINING SCHOOL

He reported for Underwater Demolition Training School (UDT) in Coronado, California on June 1, 1951. He graduated in October. He was attached to UDT 1 and joined the team assigned to Korea. By this time

Bob Weller wearing his U.S. Navy UDT diving mask. His collection of rare Spanish pieces of eight are on the wall.

Weller, a full Lieutenant, became First Division Officer, training officer, intelligence officer, then Executive Officer.

Weller was stationed at Camp McGill outside Yokosuka south of Yokohama, Japan. Camp McGill was the Underwater Demolition Team's base of operations for the Korean War.

"Louis Gibson was a high school buddy. He wrote me a letter addressed to Lieutenant Robert 'Frogfoot' Weller. Our Yeoman who handed out the mail hollered out Frogfoot all over Camp McGill for mail call. By the time he got to me with the letter everyone was calling me Frogfoot, Frogfoot. The name stuck."

"That's how Frogfoot got his name. When I started writing books about sunken treasure, I thought nobody would remember Weller but they would remember Frogfoot so I used the nickname."

KOREAN WAR DUTY

Weller spent two UDT tours of duty in Korea from 1951 to 1953. It was an inhospitable place and presented many challenges for UDT swimmers. There were many losses in combat and no clear-cut victories. UDT 1's mission was threefold. "We did surveys of beaches for possible invasion routes, we cleared offshore areas of mines and obstacles and conducted reconnaissance of areas to report on enemy activity."

Korea was so cold that when UDT 1 was assigned to survey a beach some ten miles south of Siberia they had to break ice to do it. Weller and

Lieutenant Commander Bob Weller with his UDT team in Korea fishing a dead body out of the water. U.S. NAVY, PHOTO COURTESY OF BOB WELLER.

the team worked behind enemy lines. On Korea's West Coast tides were thirty-eight feet. Boats were left high and dry with each outgoing tide.

"The water would rip through there at fifteen- to twenty knots. The land beyond is very mountainous. The men of UDT 1 were equipped with primitive dive gear by today's standards."

"The Navy never had a dry suit," Weller laughed. "They clamped in the back. We had to clamp each other into them. They always leaked and you had water running down your crack. They were always cold. They were always wet."

"We were issued a very primitive face mask," Weller pointed to his Navy dive mask on a shelf in his office. It was a round black rubber mask.

"They issued fins made of hard rubber that gouged your feet. The fins put blisters across the top of your feet. We wore canvas reef shoes to keep our feet from getting cut on coral."

"We didn't use tanks except on special assignments. Scuba tanks were very new. We used triple sixty cubic foot steel tanks with U.S. Divers regulators."

Symbol of Lieutenant Commander Bob Weller's UDT team in Korea.

"We couldn't use the steel tanks in Wonsan Harbor because of magnetic mines. Finally, they sent us aluminum tanks with beryllium fittings. The steel tanks would have set off the mines."

Like all combat personnel, UDT found ways to cope with inadequacies of issued equipment. "We wrapped our small arms in a plastic bag and stuck them into our dry suit. We'd almost have to take our dry suit off to get at the small arm but that was the way it was. We couldn't swim into the beach with a small arm and expect it to work. We had a standard GI issue knife. UDT was issued a .38 small arm. We never used those. We'd buy our own. I bought a Colt .38 on a .45 frame. At least I could hit something with that," Weller said.

COMBAT BEHIND ENEMY LINES

Navy Underwater Demolition Teams had a number of combat missions to perform, many of them only because there wasn't anyone else to do the jobs until later in the war. The east coast of Korea was a highway of roads and railroads that hugged the coastline as mountains rose sometimes from the beaches. Because of the mountainous terrain, the railroads and highways had a series of tunnels and bridges that connected the Siberian border with the city of Pusan at the southern terminal.

The air force attempted to interrupt North Korean logistics by bombing these bridges. They had little or no success against the tunnels. After a while, North Koreans began to build the repaired railroad lines in the shadows of the bridges. By running their trains only after dark and without lights were they able to keep supplies and troops heading south. It became the job of the Underwater Demolition Teams to blow up these

Lieutenant Commander Bob Weller briefing his men in Korea. U.S. NAVY, PHOTO COURTESY OF BOB WELLER.

bridges and destroy the tunnels in order to prevent troops and supplies from reaching the front lines.

One of Bob's first actions with UDT-1 was with a small group working their way inland almost a mile carrying forty pounds of plastic explosives in two haversacks, along with demolition cord and igniters. The bridge had been hit several times by the Air Force. New railroad tracks had been replaced in the shadow of the bridge. The tunnel immediately south of the bridge had never been hit after repeated attempts by fighter-bombers. The objective that night was to take out both the tunnel and the railroad.

The tunnel was guarded by North Korean civilians with rifles. The guards disappeared soon after the frogmen ordered them to "run for your lives." The tunnel and railroad were packed with explosives, and timers were set. UDT-1 members were on their way back to the beach when the charges went off. Air photos the following morning indicated it would be awhile before the Koreans could pass trucks or trains through that area again. The process would be repeated several times before a Marine Reconnaissance Group took over the job.

Then there were the mines anchored just under the surface of the water to keep ships from entering various harbors or offshore areas. What complicated the clearing of these mines was poor visibility of the waters around Korea. The tide rose or fell as much as thirty-eight feet causing a tidal current that ran 15–20 knots at times.

Mines had to be cleared. One method was to fly the area in a helicopter and watch for "swirls" in the water as the tide went in or out. This would indicate an object just below the surface. A buoy would be dropped locating the mine.

Korean mine layers would always lay a string of eight mines, that's the capacity of a thirty-two-foot mine laying canoe. When the team found one, they knew there were seven more close by. Then using slack tide to approach, UDT swimmers would attach a two pound plastic charge of C-3 to the face of the mine, run a primer cord extension to the surface, then tie in all eight mines to a single detonating cord.

A fifteen-minute timer was used to get everyone out of the water before the charges were fired. In Wonsan Harbor alone there were over 200 known mines moored just below the surface. Enemy guns were trained on every movement directed towards their removal. It wasn't the most desired duty during the war, but UDT got the job done.

Combat situations and penetration behind enemy lines was perilous in the Korean war. There were also some lighter moments. Bob Weller preferred to remember the camaraderie and situations that later on turned out to be funny. Combat veterans share Bob's view that war causes harsh memories that last forever.

"It is the hardest thing you can do. To take a train to Chicago and tell parents their son was killed in combat." Weller shook his head. The memory shut him down for a moment. He looked at his hands, folded in his lap. "I don't want to talk about it."

KOREA—SECOND TOUR OF DUTY

He wouldn't discuss the really bad times. What he enjoyed relating were anecdotes. "On the second trip over to Korea I was a full Lieutenant aboard *Wantuck*. It was an Auxiliary Personnel Destroyer. We were assigned to do a survey on a beach on the West Coast of Korea inside enemy territory well above the 38th parallel. Our job was to survey the beach for enemy activity."

When Frogfoot launched the story a glimmer in his eyes and animation in his face gave it away as a tale that was going to have some fun or mischief in it.

"It was October 1952. The sea was flat calm. Water temperature was probably sixty and visibility about four feet. I laid out the mission in the briefing room in *Wantuck*'s hold. We'd have two designated advance swimmers. Third Class Gunner's Mate Ertle volunteered for one and I volunteered for the other. I told the men at the briefing that the Chinese were in the war with trained underwater swimmers just like us" Weller said.

"Our objective was to go within five hundred yards of the beach in two separate LCPR boats. These were high-speed drop and pick up personnel boats. We started about 10 o'clock and our goal was to finish at midnight. We picked moonless nights."

"The two LCPRs were 500 yards apart. They dropped Ertle and I and we swam into the beach five hundred yards apart. The *Wantuck* stayed off about seven miles. Our objective was to swim into the beach, then swim toward each other and swim out together when we met."

Weller used his hands for emphasis. Arthritis in his fingers caused them to bend at an angle when he separated his fingers. His work hardened; strong hands always added drama to his stories.

"I took the south and Ertle took the north. The beach was on an island that was two hundred yards wide, maybe three-quarters of a mile long and it lay two hundred yards off the mainland that provided a mountainous backdrop."

"As I approached the beach, I saw this big mountain in front of me. I swam toward it as a landmark. I didn't realize I was so close to the beach until my elbows and legs started touching. At night distance will fool ya."

"The mountain turned out to be a dead goat. I didn't know it was a goat until I swam right into it. It smelled to high heaven. It was bloated, washed up onto the beach and had been there some time," Weller laughed.

"Ertle was coming in on the north side of the beach. He knew from my briefing that the Chinese had underwater swimmers. Ertle saw a head come up in front of him. It came out of the water. He took a couple of strokes toward it and whispered, 'Is that you Mister Weller?' Suddenly the head disappeared and Ertle could see a phosphorescent trail swimming underwater."

"The head appeared on the other side of him about fifteen feet away. Ertle swam toward it and whispered again, 'Is that you Mister Weller?' Ertle didn't know whether to abandon his mission and swim back to the boat or to continue. The head appeared directly in front of him about ten feet away for a third time. He asked it distinctly 'Is that you Mister Weller?' It barked at him as only a seal can bark. He continued the mission."

When Weller and Ertle met up at the center of the beach, the Gunner's Mate couldn't wait to tell him the story. Weller also had a tale to tell but they waited until they rejoined the pick-up boats and were safely away from the beach. "Everybody had a good laugh."

Weller spent two tours in Korea. He was discharged from the Navy with a Purple Heart, a handful of medals, and the rank of Lieutenant Commander in February 1954.

TAMPA, FLORIDA

"My stepfather and mother were living in Gulfport, Florida near Tampa. We moved down. I was still married to my first wife Pat and had two kids. I was looking for a job in Florida. I couldn't get a job as an architect. I wrote all the powder companies. I was a demolition man. Atlas Powder hired me as a lab technician."

UNIVERSITY OF DELAWARE

He transferred to Hercules Powder Company and worked as a janitor for three years. It was near the University of Delaware where he enrolled and earned a Civil Engineering degree.

Bob's new surroundings would form friendships that would last long after graduation. He founded the Delaware Underwater Swim Club in 1954. He and a group of friends began diving shipwrecks off Delaware's coast.

The strain of work and study "Was harder on my wife and kids than it was on me. I worked 7 days a week. I said to my wife, 'You can pick where you want to live after graduation.' I accepted a job with Honeywell and we moved to Tampa, Florida. Within a month of being hired, Honeywell sent me to school in Philadelphia and transferred me to Greensboro, North Carolina. Honeywell promised to ship me permanently to Florida when they had their first opening."

WORK WITH HONEYWELL

Weller became Honeywell's top salesman. "I did 1043% of my quota. I spent two-and-a-half years in Greensboro. They hired two salesmen down in Florida and never gave me a shot at it. I was having lunch in an open-air shopping mall in Durham. They were playing 'The Girl From Ipanema.' I walked to the car and thought that there was no reason for me to be in Greensboro when I want to work and play in Florida."

He walked into the Honeywell office and told his boss that he was going to Florida with or without Honeywell as of July first. A meeting was arranged with the Regional Vice-President in Honeywell's Atlanta office. "They asked at that meeting whether the Regional Manager promised I'd be sent to Florida. I said yes. Within two weeks the Regional Manager was fired."

"In May 1960, the new regional manager sat down with me. He said he didn't like people who threatened his company. I said I didn't care, 'You didn't keep your promise.' He said July first you will be in Miami."

Weller became the Industrial Manager for Honeywell's Miami office on 1 July 1960. He remained with Honeywell in Miami for the next ten years.

"I was there two weeks before I bought my first boat," Weller smiled again. "It was a sixteen-foot plywood boat on a trailer powered by a 35 horsepower Johnson motor. I called it *Frogfoot*."

2

FROGFOOT—THE BOAT

*F*ROGFOOT WAS ON A TRAILER. THE BOAT GAVE BOB AND HIS friends the ability to go anywhere in the Florida Keys. The trouble was, Weller didn't know where any of the shipwrecks were.

"About that time Harry Wiseman, my Mechanical Engineering professor at the University of Delaware, along with two other professors Vohnnie Pearson and Art Jarvella made good on their promise."

Weller taught his professors how to dive, while attending university, in the YMCA pool. They had all been diving with him on shipwrecks off Delaware's coast.

"A month before I graduated, we all met in Dr. Wiseman's office. The professors announced that when I graduated, they were going to leave the University of Delaware and come to Florida with me and dive," Weller recalled.

"I laughed. It was kind of a joke but they were dead serious. Sure enough, when Honeywell finally transferred me to Miami, Harry Wiseman came down and got a job at the Mechanical Engineering Department of the University of Miami. Art Jarvella came down and was courted by Maurice Connel, a mechanical engineering firm. Vohnnie Pearson came to Florida and got a job at Pratt and Whitney."

THE PROFESSOR JOINS WELLER DIVING

Weller just settled in Florida. His friend and former professor Harry Wiseman began teaching at the University of Miami. "I stopped by his new house. Harry's wife told me Harry was driving a cab part time. I said, 'You're kidding.' He had to pay some bills off on the new house they bought."

Weller called the cab company and found out Harry was parked in front of the Dupont Hotel on Miami's waterfront. "I drove down, parked, found the cab and got in the back door." Weller was always ready for fun. Playing a good joke characterized his personality. He had an open, friendly personality and liked to laugh.

"Harry had not seen me in almost three years. I said, 'What are you waiting for?' Harry turned around in surprise."

That weekend Weller and Wiseman were in the water behind Molasses Reef Light out of Key Largo. "We swam through the breakers of the reef not realizing the place was full of sharks. We never did that again. It was my first week there and it was the First of July."

Because of his naval service, Weller and Wiseman were about the same age. "I was the oldest graduate at the University of Delaware in 1957. The people at the University treated Korean War vets right. I got out of Korea and was still limping around."

With *Frogfoot* on a trailer Weller and Wiseman were diving for treasure in the Keys every weekend. They were halcyon days.

"There were days you felt like you owned the whole ocean. The water was crystal clear, calm. I'd stand on the bow of the boat, Harry would drive. Some days I could spot the wrecks two hundred yards away. Sometimes the ocean made you fight for every inch."

For a moment Weller relaxed into his soft leather chair, savored hot coffee, and looked around his living room. It was winter in Florida. A log crackled in the fireplace. The walls and shelves, cabinets and bookcases were crowded with artifacts recovered from the deep.

"The ocean was something you became very personal with. You took what it was willing to give you and you were thankful for it." Another sip of coffee and Weller was back in the water, diving Conch Reef that first week with his friend Harry Wiseman off Key Largo.

"A couple of hundred yards from the buoy were square blocks of granite. Building blocks probably being taken to Fort Jefferson in the Dry Tortugas. The wreck looked like it was from the 1800s. We were picking up bronze spikes," Weller said.

FIRST ENCOUNTER WITH TREASURE DIVER CRAIG HAMILTON

"A Marine Patrol boat came alongside. In those days the Marine Patrol guys were very friendly. He wanted to know how we were doing. We told him that there were big moray eels and spiny sea urchins and we'd found some spikes."

The Marine Patrolman pointed off down the reef. "A couple of divers are on a wreck and picking up coins about two miles there."

Weller laughed. "We said thank you. As soon as he pulled off, we pulled our anchor up and headed down the reef. That's when I met Craig Hamilton."

"There were two boats anchored over the *El Infante* in sixteen feet of water. When we pulled up and anchored a diver came to the surface and got in his boat. It was Craig Hamilton. He was one of the first divers in the Keys after Art McKee."

Hamilton offered Weller a cup of coffee. Weller asked what the divers were finding. "Cob coins. At the time I didn't know what a cob coin was. I asked if Craig knew the name of the shipwreck. He said the *Infante* that sank in 1733. He'd been diving on it several years."

Craig Hamilton turned out to be a neighbor of the Wellers in South Miami. He was a fireman and shift worker so had the ability to get days off to dive shipwrecks in the Keys. Weller took him up on an offer to visit and see artifacts they were finding.

"Craig had a lot of great stuff. He had a 1732 pillar dollar. A beautiful coin. He became my mentor. Craig showed me how to put together an airlift. We used an Eastern Airlines air conditioning air pump. He showed me how to put a breathing compressor together."

Weller dove with Hamilton. "After a couple of months, I got my own equipment together. Harry Wiseman and I were ready to do it on our own."

Weller had become interested in making underwater movies. While filming Craig on the *El Infante* site, Craig cut a trench on the bottom with the airlift. The suction device sent compressed air down a pipe that created a venturi at the end enabling divers to work it back and forth on a sandy bottom literally vacuuming the sand away underwater.

"When you get through with your movie thing you work one side of the trench, I'll work the other," Craig had told Weller on the boat.

"I was down filming Craig. He stopped suddenly, reached down and picked up a gold earring in the shape of a cross with three emeralds in it. Four emeralds were missing. Craig came over and waved it in front of my nose like that." Weller motioned with his fingers imitating Hamilton's wiggling the earring in front of him.

"I surfaced, threw the camera in the boat, grabbed an airlift and headed for the bottom. I found a double banded gold wedding ring that day." It was Frogfoot's gold treasure christening.

Craig told him that in the three years he'd been working the *El Infante* site he hadn't found a gold ring. "And you do it on your first try."

"That started it. There's something about finding your first piece of gold that turns you on. It made a treasure finder out of me." Weller explored the *El Infante* site every weekend. He found cob coins that had been clipped from a flat bar of silver then trimmed by hand to the proper weight and stamped with the impressions of the Spanish mint.

"I found buckles and buttons, two more gold rings, a gold medallion with images of Saint Josef and Saint Anne on it."

Weller dove on the forward reef face in about thirty feet of water. "We ran into bronze that came off the HMS *Fly* that sank in 1805. A big Jewfish came in and was tailing us, very curious."

Weller wrote to the British Museum in London. The divers wanted a chart that showed the sinking of HMS *Fly*. "As it turned out Captain Pelew's crew was drunk when the *Fly* ran aground on the reef."

MAP OF TREASURE FLEET

Weller received a reply from the museum listing charts they had available in the files. "They had forty charts. One that stood out was the 1733 fleet. I called the museum in London and asked how I could get a copy of that 1733 fleet chart. The woman said, 'We are going to have to charge for that but we can make you a copy.' I asked how much? 'It will cost you the equivalent of fifty cents.' I sent her $5. It wound up to be a total of five charts and this was the first one."

This proved to be a breakthrough Hamilton and Weller had been waiting for. "When we got that chart only the *El Infante*, *Capitana El Rubi*, *San Pedro* and *Almirante Gallo Indiana* of the 1733 fleet, sunk in a hurricane in the Florida Keys, had been located. There were a total of twenty-one ships. That left a wide-open field for discovery."

3

EXPLORING THE 1733 FLEET

Chart of the location of Spanish shipwrecks in hand, the small team of divers began finding new sites. "Finding an intact and unsalvaged virgin shipwreck of the 1733 fleet was unreal." Frogfoot remembered with excitement.

"Each wreck had different things on it. Even though most had been salvaged by the Spanish, cargoes had been scattered. There was very little gold on the 1733 fleet. The Spanish got most of it. There was not much silver," he added.

Weller and Hamilton were finding new shipwrecks. They worked secretly since other salvage divers were in the Keys looking for the same galleons.

"We didn't try to make a big deal about our discoveries. We kept it to ourselves." They worked the 1733 fleet from 1960 to 1964.

"By 1964 we located all of the ships except the *San Jose*, *San Fernando*, *El Populo* and the *San Ignacio*."

1964 STATE MORATORIUM

"In 1964, the State of Florida stepped in. They put a moratorium on diving. No one could dive without a lease. The moratorium lasted until 1965. Everybody was out of the water until the State awarded ten leases. They kept the number to ten because that was the number of inspectors they would hire to stay aboard each salvage boat."

"Most of the leases were politically motivated. Fifty-four salvors requested leases. I was one of them. Each had experience. Yet only two were issued leases by the State: Treasure Salvors, the Mel Fisher group, and Real Eight. The rest went to people who never dove before. We got none," Weller declared.

THE FIRST MEETING WITH MEL FISHER

"That's a good one," Bob said. He cleared his throat, took a sip of cherry-cranberry flavored juice. He thought a moment before he described how he first met the legendary Mel Fisher.

"Mel came down in sixty-four. In sixty-five, working with Kip Wagner on the 1715 fleet, they had recovered quite a bit of treasure. They had a big display planned at the Fountainbleu Hotel in Miami Beach. About the time we were salvaging the 1733 fleet," Bob said.

In 1965, Weller formed a corporation called Royal Fifth with friends Brad Patten, Pat Patterson, and Ray Manieri.

He took another drink from the tall glass, savored the juice, put it back on a large rattan, glass-topped table on the veranda of his house facing a canal, interlaced his two hands and braced them against the back of his head. It was a Weller trademark. It marked a good tale in the offing.

"Craig Hamilton, who got me into this to begin with met Bob Paige, a man from New York. Bob Paige, through people he knew in New York was able to make reproductions of some of the coins Craig was finding. They used the reproductions for tie tacks, key chains and the like," Bob said.

"I had found a nice, full dated 1731 one real coin from the *San Pedro*. It was a very nice coin. I thought I could get some reproductions made and make tie tacks. I'd written Bob Paige in New York a letter telling him what I had and asked if he could get some repros made."

His recollection was going back more than forty years. He seemed to savor it as the memory came back this warm, spring afternoon sitting amidst Margaret's elaborate and cherished orchids. They hung everywhere from veranda beams. Amazing orchids in all shapes and bizarre colors, one a peppermint candy striped white and red in full bloom. The orchid was directly in front of where Bob was sitting with his cold drink.

"Paige called me. He said he was coming down to the Fisher display at the Fountainbleu the following week and to meet him there. Imagine a ballroom full of people. A huge display. Gold and silver that had never been displayed before."

"I walked up to a man I thought was Mel Fisher and I introduced myself. He was very cordial. 'Oh, you're a treasure diver too. Oh, that's great,' Mel said. He introduced me to a guy standing next to him. That man was Bob Paige," Weller related.

"Paige pulled a letter out of his pocket. 'I'm supposed to meet you here today,' he said. That's right I told Paige. I pulled out this beautiful, full dated reale coin I'd found. Everybody passed it around. They said, 'That's great.'" Weller recounted the incident.

"Paige said he could get reproductions made. While we were standing around looking at the coin a heavy man with a bag in his hand walked up. It was Frank Allen, Vice President of Treasure Salvors, Mel's company. Frank said, 'Let me see that coin. That's a great coin. You're really proud of that coin?' I said yes, I am. Frank opened the bag he was carrying and said, 'Hold out your hand.' He promptly dropped five uncleaned pieces of eight into my hand."

"Frank was going around giving out pieces of eight to publicize Mel's find. After I got done ooing and ahhing and said thank you very much, I said, 'Frank I got one problem.'"

Weller smiled, unwrapped his hands from behind his neck, sipped his cherry-cranberry juice and remembered the story as vividly as if it had occurred that afternoon.

"'What's that?' Frank asked me. I said there are four of us in my group of divers, the Royal Fifth. How can I divide five coins among four of us? Frank thought for a moment, said 'Hold out your hand,' and dropped seven more pieces of eight in my hand. 'That's twelve. That should do it.' I said yes and thank you very much." Weller looked delighted with the telling of the tale that brought him his first contact with Mel Fisher.

Frank Allen and Weller became close friends over time. Mel Fisher invited Bob to come up to dive with him on Kip Wagner's shipwrecks from the 1715 fleet. "They'd found a big pile on the *Nieves*."

WORKING WITH MEL FISHER

Mel Fisher, with his state lease in hand, set up a company in Marathon called Armada Research. Fisher put Dick Williams in charge.

"Dick's primary diver was Bobby Jordan. Using magnetometers, they were able to locate twenty-seven wrecks in the Keys. They never found any significant treasure after a year of diving."

"One of the wrecks I visited with them was the Christmas Tree Wreck. The site had piles of cannons and bar shot all over. The wreck got its name from the fact that when they went out magging and got a hit they would drop a green marker buoy. They ran out of green and started dropping red buoys. Dick went out one day and said it looks like a Christmas Tree," Weller explained.

"That wreck lay five-hundred yards from the old beacon that had been knocked down on Coffins Patch. For a long time, we thought that was the site of the *San Ignacio*. We found 1732 and 1733 pillar dollars on the site. It was five miles offshore in sixteen feet of water." "There was a huge mound of ballast on the wreck site with ten-foot-long cannons all over the place. We began finding axe heads, a box of sail needles, hammer heads, and sailor's palms. With these finds we felt that no ship would be going back to Spain carrying these items that would have been destined for the New World."

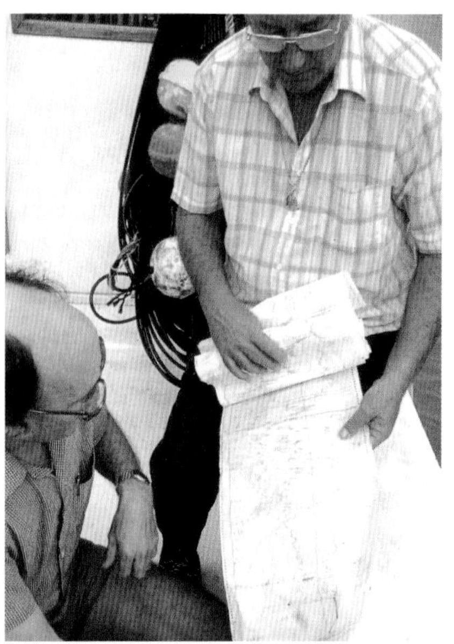

Mel Fisher (standing) with engineering wizard Fay Feild studying printout made towing a magnetometer under water behind Fisher's search boat.

The wreck site they were working was likely that of the *Situato*, an armed merchant ship that accompanied the 1733 fleet and was heading for St. Augustine, Florida. "One survivor came ashore on a plank at Craig's Key. We wondered why we were finding pillar dollars on this wreck. We decided it was the payroll for the soldiers in St. Augustine. That means the *San Ignacio* is still out there. We don't know where it is."

"I'd been approached by a real estate salesman who sold me my house in Green Hills, South Miami. His name was Al Greenberg. Al saw some of the artifacts in my guestroom when he was checking our pool patio. We had water standing in the patio after every rain."

"My second wife Gladys, I called her Gigi, told Al that 'Bob is a treasure diver.' Al had two buddies Manuel Sirkin and Norman Somberg. Somberg was a lawyer and Manny owned Army and Navy stores in Miami."

OUTSIDE STATE JURIDICTION

Al told Gigi to tell Bob that if he needed an investment to give his two pals a call. "So I called. I told them we can work the wrecks outside the three-mile limit. The *Infante* was outside the three-mile limit. We had a meeting at my house between Royal Fifth and the potential investors."

"The meeting started about 7 o'clock at night. We sat around my dining room table in Green Hills. Somberg, the lawyer, came to that meeting to shoot me down. These men had invested in a treasure operation about two years before, lost several thousand dollars. Got zilch." Bob recalled the meeting.

"When they sat down at the table the first question I asked was, 'Why do you want to throw your money away in a treasure diving project?' Norman Somberg confided in me later that that blew the wind out of his sails. The more the investors heard, the more they listened."

Bob revealed the situation with the State of Florida. They could work the *Infante* site. Craig Hamilton and Weller had already found nice artifacts near the turn of the hull of the *Capitana* but nobody had searched under the turn of the hull of the *Infante*. By the end of the night Weller and his group had the investment.

THE *BIG FISHERMAN*

"They asked us how much we'll need. We said $6000. That was our first investment. With that we bought a suspect 32-foot scuba charter boat called the *Big Fisherman*. The engines were gone, that's why the guy sold it. The boat cost $3000. We bought an airlift and a breathing compressor and a five horsepower Hale fire pump and we went diving."

It wasn't quite that simple. Pat Patterson and Bob Weller took the *Big Fisherman* from Crandall Park Marina in Miami down to Key Largo. Coming through a narrow pass Bob ran *Big Fisherman* up on sandbanks at a place called Mosquito Banks. They got it off.

"Our wives had driven down and were waiting for us to dock. Pat Patterson and I were up on the flying bridge bringing it through the breakwater. The wind picked up to fifteen knots from the North. I had a horn up on the bridge. I blew it for all it was worth for our wives. Just as we came through the breakwater the port engine shut down."

Everyone was watching. "Trying to back into a slip with one engine and the wind against you was almost impossible. Our wives were so embarrassed that we didn't know how to run that boat that they disappeared. Finally, the little old lady that ran the marina threw us a line and dragged us stern first into the dock."

"That was the beginning of our salvage project." It took them three weeks to put *Big Fisherman* into running condition and fit it out. The men were enthusiastic. "We found ourselves running down the dock just to get a can of oil. Even though the treasure had been there three-hundred years we felt we could not wait."

"Finally, we got everything ready. It was a Sunday. We invited the investors and their wives and kids, the divers and their wives and kids aboard the boat. We took *Big Fisherman* behind Rodriguez Island. The sandy bottom was six feet deep, water was crystal clear. Everybody went swimming. I sat up on the flying bridge and thought 'It can't get any better than this.'" Weller smiled, recalling the launching of their new treasure-hunting project.

"We were ready to go diving on a big scale. We got on the *Infante* around May 1965, and we began working under the hull. We found a silver piece of four and a gold link to a chain. Otherwise, it was disappointing."

"We worked the *Infante* the better part of four weeks. We looked around the area. We were finding silver buckles, a few coins. Nothing like we had expected," Weller said. "We nearly sank the *Big Fisherman*," he laughed. "I have to hedge a little here." Bob got the look of mischief in his eyes.

"We had a license to use dynamite out there. . . ." Weller now thought better of the statement he was about to make. It attributed the leak in *Big Fisherman*'s stern to his demolition expertise or, more likely, the lapse in time between his UDT service using explosives and years in civilian life.

LEAKING BOAT

". . . Well, we developed a leak in the stern. As we were rounding Little Conch Reef the boat felt a little sluggish. Manieri checked the engine and said, 'Bob we're sinking.' If you want a bone chilling statement, have someone tell you your boat is sinking. We were a good distance from shore. I opened both engines. I felt if we could make it to Rodriguez Island, we could salvage the gear. Rodriguez Island was eight miles away," he said.

"We made it past the island and just into our dock. I jumped over the side and saw we had almost a half-inch gap in the stern planking. With a cloth and screwdriver, I plugged it. We fired up the Hale fire pump and pumped the water out of the stern. We just barely made it."

Big Fisherman was hauled at Marathon and repaired. Patched and back in the water the team was operational again. Bob called Mel Fisher. Mel was living in Vero Beach at the time still working the Spanish 1715 fleet.

DINNER WITH MEL FISHER

"I said, Mel, let me come up and spring for dinner. My second wife Gladys and I drove up. We took Mel and his wife Deo, and his electronic wizard Fay Feild to dinner at the Driftwood Inn. Afterwards we went discoing until about one in the morning. At one in the morning, me and Gladys, who I called Gigi, Deo and Mel were walking on the beach," Weller explained.

"I told Mel I have a salvage boat fully equipped. I have divers that know what they're doing. I need a shipwreck so I don't disappoint our investors. We're not finding what we're looking for on the *Infante*."

"Mel said 'I'll be glad to share a wreck with ya. I'll call Dick Williams and tell him to give you a wreck. We have 27 of them down there.'"

Weller was still working full time at Honeywell. He was working the shipwrecks in the Keys on weekends. The next weekend he drove

Mel Fisher with his famous gold chain found on a Spanish galleon.

to Conch Key and met Dick Williams. Dick told Weller that they thought they had located a wreck they believed to be the *Sueco de Arizon* about three hundred yards off Duck Key.

The wreck site was buoyed with red Clorox bottles. Briefly worked by the Fisher group they found one piece of four on the site and Williams and Fisher did not expect to find much more.

"When you weekenders get through with this wreck I'll give you another one," Williams told Weller.

"Dick Williams was an egotistical person. He had boxes of gold coins as his share of the division from recoveries made on the 1715 fleet. He showed them to us. I told Dick, 'If there is anything on that wreck site, we'll find it.'"

WORKING A BALLAST PILE

Weller and his team started working the next weekend. It was the first week in June 1965.

"We worked four weekends on this 80' x 30' x 4' high ballast pile. We systematically moved every ballast stone."

The divers first found ceramic and pottery shards and other artifacts until 1 July 1965. "July first always seems to be a lucky day." Weller began the tale.

"We narrowed the ballast pile down to 5' x 15'. It was 4 o'clock in the afternoon. Pat Patterson had broken a couple of ribs when he got thumped down on a ballast pile so he was not in the water. Brad Patten was in the cabin worn out after a long day. Ray and I were in the water."

"I'd been working to dig out a K'ang Hsi cup. It turned out to be broken. I swam over to the other side of the ballast pile to where Ray was working. I showed him the cup and said I'm going up. He came up to the surface with me. Ray said, 'Bob I've got five pieces of eight.'"

Ray dug the coins out of a yellow ski jacket he wore underwater to keep warm and handed them to Weller.

"Ray said tell the guys not to shut the compressor down. When the guys got tired of waiting for us they would shut the compressor down to get us to come up," Weller explained. It was getting late in the afternoon.

Weller swam to the stern of *Big Fisherman*, handed up the finds and told the men aboard to keep the compressor running. "We hit it," Weller told them then disappeared below again.

Brad and Pat scrambled to pick up the five pieces of eight Weller had dropped on the stern. When Bob swam down and joined Ray below, there was a big pile of silver coins waiting to be picked up.

"I brought them up to the surface. Brad Patten jumped over the side. No face mask, no fins. He wanted to take a look at what was going on."

Brad borrowed Weller's gear and went down to pick up the next bucket of silver pieces of eight off the bottom.

They were running low on fuel. Weller transferred gasoline out of the boat's fuel tank to the compressor engine to keep it running.

"It was 7 o'clock. It got dark and we had to go in. There were coins everywhere. We covered what we could see with ballast stones, pulled our anchor and headed for the dock at Duck Key. That was 1 July 1965."

Weller's signal to their wives if ever they hit it big was to lower the dive flag to half-mast.

"Somewhere between the dive site and the dock I dropped the dive flag to half-mast. We came up the channel and saw the girls on the dock. I was on the flying bridge and raised a fist in the air then pulled alongside the dock. Pat Patterson said that he'd call his wife from the marina to tell her that we hit it. He jumped off and went to the public phone booth a hundred yards up the dock."

BUCKETS OF COINS AND A LOOSE BOAT

"I jumped down off the flying bridge, picked Gigi up and swung her around. We had three buckets of coins in the cabin. I ran up to the phone booth to call the investors for a celebration."

"I turned around from the phone booth to walk back to the boat. It was drifting away. Nobody tied it to the dock." Weller jumped into the water, swam to *Big Fisherman* and brought it back.

"I had been draining gas out of the fuel tank to run the compressor. By the time we got to the dock a long-legged fly could have walked around in the gas tank and not drown," he laughed.

Weller and the crew cleaned up the boat. They put the buckets of coins in the trunk of his Buick convertible. Their wives drove back to Miami. By the time Weller arrived home the party was in full swing. The investors brought bottles of champagne.

"I had a pool in Green Hills with a patio bar. All the coins were dumped on the bar. There were several clearly dated 1732 pillar dollars. It was a very valuable coin worth a couple of thousand dollars."

Weller went back to work at Honeywell the next day, a Monday. "For the first three days the phone wouldn't stop ringing. "The investors would call and ask, 'How rich are we?' The divers would call and ask, 'How many coins do you think are left on the wreck?' Questions, questions."

The next weekend was July Fourth. The men were off Thursday and Friday. They booked three rooms at the Christianson Motel in Marathon. The divers were up late the night before planning how they would explore the wreck site to insure they found all the coins.

"We were on site at 6 AM. The ballast pile was just as we left it. Just the thought that under the rocks were all those coins was driving us crazy." The divers laid out yellow ski ropes on the bottom to form a search grid. The grid was fifty feet all around the area.

"The first thing I saw that day were two pillar dollars stuck together. I very carefully pried them off the bottom. The date 1732 was very pronounced. There was bar shot with coins stuck to it. There were seven of us working the bottom. We were getting in each other's way."

It was a family jaunt. The investors' sons would dive down with a bucket in water only eight feet deep. "We'd fill up a bucket with coins and they'd bring it up. Up and down with buckets of coins. By 3 o'clock in the afternoon we were finished."

BIG FIND—BIG NEWS

Weller and the team knew they had quite a haul of valuable shipwreck coins. "We were faced with a dilemma publicity wise. We called the *Miami Herald.* They asked us to bring the coins in. The next day we had a half-page spread about the big treasure find. We were sitting around a table with a big pile of coins."

Coins discovered underwater were often clumped together. Here two gold "Escudos" remain attached to a lump of silver pieces of eight.

"Mel Fisher called me. He said, 'Bob, I'm supposed to be in charge of all publicity. What's this about the coins?' We jumped the gun a little bit."

The exploration of the *Sueco de Arizon* was finished. Weller and the team turned all the coins in to Mel Fisher. Seven months later a division with the State of Florida took place in Gainesville where the archaeological conservation laboratory was located. The lab was to clean the coins.

"We had photographs of twelve pillar dollars. Only ten showed up. One other coin we knew we had wasn't there until they produced it from another cleaning room." Weller made it clear that he was suspect of state conduct.

The State received 25 percent off the top. Mel Fisher received 50 percent of what was left and the Weller group received 50 percent.

"I took two 1732 pillar dollars and a few silver pieces of eight. The divers and backers split the rest. The investors got several hundred coins each," he said.

The agreement with the investors was that they would put up $6,000 for the first season since equipment had to be purchased then $3,000 the next year for gas and oil and operating money. Fisher offered the Weller group other wreck sites to work.

"We all had jobs so we were working the shipwrecks on weekends only. At work I suddenly got a call from the marina that *Big Fisherman* was sinking. By the time I drove down to Marathon, *Big Fisherman* was sitting on the bottom."

The pump stopped working and the batteries were dead. Weller hired the Shurgar Brothers to raise the dive boat and dry out the engine. With their cash depleted on repairs, the 1966 season ended.

4

MARGARET ANN MATHEWS

Bob met Margaret Ann Mathews in 1970. They were married on June 1, 1974. Margaret was born in Pointe a Pierre, Trinidad on June 16, 1939. Her father was an English geologist who came to Trinidad to work with the oil companies. Margaret's mother was born in Trinidad of Austrian and French parents.

Margaret went to school in Caracas, Venezuela. All of her early studies were in Spanish. Her fluency in Spanish would later help with manuscript translations received from the Archives of the Indies in Seville. It wasn't until she was sent to a British school that she learned to read and write English.

Margaret went to college in the United States, first at Brenau College in Gainesville, Georgia then at Webber College in Lake Wales, Florida. After college she returned to Venezuela. When her father retired from Shell Oil Company the family moved to the United States and settled in Miami.

Margaret was married for the first time in Venezuela to William Bennett. They had two sons Alan and Robert. When they divorced Margaret moved in with her parents in Miami. Alan was five and Robert two.

"I worked for a land company. I couldn't take it. They were selling land underwater. Then I worked in a laundromat. I didn't have a car so had no transportation. Finally I went to work for the Miami Serpentarium for Bill Haast," Margaret recounted.

Bob and Margaret Weller at home in Weller's Cove.

MARGARET AND THE SNAKES

The job suited her. She learned every aspect of the work. "I did everything. I'd clean the snake pits, clean the crock pits, give guided tours. I did venom extractions with Bill Haast. I ran the gift shop and did the buying."

Margaret was a diver and underwater photographer when she met Bob. "I knew a couple of guys. One was an underwater photographer. I like the outdoors and diving was something I always wanted to do. I took scuba lessons in Miami in 1969."

Bob laughed when he recalled Margaret's job at the Serpentarium. "I saved her from a bunch of snakes," he said.

But the match didn't start off at the first meeting, didn't even seem likely at first. At least in Margaret's eyes.

"I was working in the gift shop. We used to sell reproductions of Spanish coins. Bob's company made them into necklaces, key chains and the like. They were good sellers and we were out of merchandise and had no way to get in touch with him." Margaret paused.

She sat on a leather sofa in the TV den, one bare foot on a hatch cover coffee table set with shipwreck coins, many gold escudo reproductions from Bob's old company.

"One day he walked into the gift shop. I put in a large order. He asked me out. I turned him down," Margaret mused.

"I told one of the girls in the Serpentarium." Margaret's Trinidadian lilt was evident as she described the ensuing conversation with her coworker.

"What you tell him?" The coworker asked Margaret.

"No. I told him no. I don't like his nose," Margaret said to her girlfriend.

"If he wants to spend some bread on you, let him spend some bread on you," the coworker advised. That was in 1970.

Bob came back to the Serpentarium several times. He asked Margaret out again and Margaret accepted. "He proposed to me in October 1973. We were married on 1 June 1974 and we've been together ever since," Margaret smiled. Her red hair, twinkling blue eyes, good nature and hospitality are legend in the community of treasure divers.

When Margaret throws a party, it is always a grand affair. Even casual tea or coffee is served on a tray with porcelain cups, saucers, and elegant flatware.

"When I met Bob, he had a boat and we would go diving with his friends on various wrecks. It was more exciting than just taking pictures. I was finding pottery shards and antique bottles," she said.

"Bob was working with Richard MacAllaster in the Keys. MacAllaster brought the operation up to Fort Pierce to work the 1715 fleet. Bob started working up there. I'd occasionally go out on our friends John and Judy Halas' boat."

NO WOMAN ABOARD

"MacAllaster didn't want women aboard his 48-foot lugger *Bamboo Bay*. I was taking care of my parents at the time and the kids were young," Margaret explained. MacAllaster eventually made an exception for Margaret.

"Back in those days I could see the small coins better than Bob. He would chase me down underwater to find them. With Wegener's disease my vision now is blurred." Recent bouts with a debilitating illness required long hospital stays and treatment at home.

AT HOME IN FLORIDA

The Weller house in Florida is located on a canal that forms a T. It is where boats in early times, loaded with produce for market, used to turn around. Large alligators sun themselves directly across from the Weller's gazebo. The waterfront deck, set with black granite counters, made of hardwoods, with stainless gas grills and large hand-blown antique glass net floaters, is a gathering place for treasure divers.

Annual week-long and long weekend seminars are held on the deck. Bob and Margaret conducted seminars about the salvage of sunken Spanish shipwrecks. Margaret continued the tradition after Bob's death. People came from all over the U.S. to learn salvage techniques, dive off a treasure boat and enjoy Margaret's gracious hospitality and delicious food.

COIN IN THE ROOF

"Look up there," Bob told visitors. Inside the cupola that holds the weathervane of the Spanish tiled gazebo roof is a Spanish piece of eight. Bob inlaid it into the wooden beam and glued it in place. It is a talisman akin to the thought of mariners of old that stepped their masts with a coin for good luck.

Jokes and good fellowship always abounded in what came to be called Weller's Cove. "We didn't have wetsuits like we have today," Margaret might joke during coffee breaks at a seminar.

"We used long johns. Bob Luyendyk used to borrow mine. There were pink flowers on them. He didn't care," Margaret laughed.

There are little stories that recall the emotion of finding treasure and the fellowship of divers working below. For all the treasure the Wellers found, it has not been the lure of gold itself, rather the challenge of adventure that kept them diving.

"I worked a lot with George Hook on the Cabin site," Margaret said. "We were finding little links of a gold chain. To get the tiny links out of the cracks in the reef we designed a wire tool so we could hook each link and pull it out. It took a half-hour just to get one link out. We were being pushed around by surge. When we finished, we had enough gold links to fill a small glass vial."

"We always worked as a team underwater. Very seldom was there only one person down. We needed one person to move rocks the other to use the metal detector," Margaret said.

Bob and Margaret made a great treasure diving team. "Bob had trouble with his ears so he would stay on the bottom once he cleared them. I would take the stuff up to the surface or take messages up to move the boat," Margaret smiled.

5

WORK WITH MACALLASTER

WELLER WAS TOO BUSY WITH HIS NEW JOB AT LAB DATA Control to do much underwater salvage until 1978. In 1978, Richard MacAllaster called him and asked if Bob would like to join them as a diver at Fort Pierce where they were going to work the 1715 Spanish plate fleet that wrecked in a hurricane off the coast.

Bob had grown children by this time. Three kids by his first wife and he adopted his second wife's only child. Margaret has two grown children. He was able to spend weekends working with MacAllaster on the 1715 fleet.

"Richard MacAllaster had a 48-foot old river boat called *Bamboo Bay*. At the time, if you got ten days on the bottom working the wreck site, you were in on the division. We were diving for the first time on the 1715 fleet," Weller said.

"MacAllaster applied for and got a state lease on the Fort Pierce site. That's where Mel Fisher made a legend for himself when he recovered over two thousand gold coins on the bottom there in 1964. Fisher recovered $5 million in gold and silver coins," Frogfoot said.

Mel Fisher moved off the wreck site in 1967. "Between 1967 and 1978 only Rex Stocker worked the site one year and Rathman worked it one year. Rathman located a cannon Mel Fisher called "Charlie" with about four thousand silver pieces of eight alongside it."

"Rathman had no idea how to work a site. He blew a hole eight feet deep. A cannon dropped into the hole. The muzzle of the cannon was just barely sticking above the surface. We started to work the site and here is this cannon barrel sticking out of the bottom."

"Nobody really knew how to work that site. It had been hit or miss. Treasure was left all over the bottom. In 1978 MacAllaster set up a circular grid pattern. He used three beach markers and would take sextant bearings on them. This allowed us to work the site meticulously foot by foot," Weller explained.

The divers working with Richard MacAllaster covered the fifty-five acre ocean site under the state lease. "That first year we picked up nine gold coins, two gold rings, maybe a thousand silver coins. That was without metal detectors. We had a sort of inauspicious salvage season in 1978 but in 1979, we really got into it with metal detectors."

GOLD

The divers were surprised by how much they were finding. "We were all still working weekends that second year. With the metal detectors we found 42 pieces of worked gold jewelry, 68 gold coins and over two thousand silver coins along with swords and pistols. It proved there was a lot of treasure left on the site."

"One day in 1979, I found 47 gold coins in one spot. It was where the ship came apart and the top deck came ashore with the captain and 105 of his crew between B and C markers. It was right where there were nine cannons. A pair of crossed anchors lay on the bottom."

Archive records indicated that *Nuestra Senora de las Nieves'* Captain, Soto Sanchez, reported that the top deck separated and washed ashore. The captain and his men stepped onto the beach. "That wasn't true but it was close enough," Bob Weller commented about the report.

The ocean bottom where the divers were working was Pleistocene. "Inshore the bottom was 30,000-year-old mangrove roots closely matted together. When we blew into it, it turned absolutely black. We would have zero visibility. Until we learned how to work in that, we were diving braille. Still, we were finding great things."

Gold coins found by the Wellers.

Gold "Escudo" bearing the Latin cross with lions symbolizing Leon and castles symbolizing Castile dominions of the Spanish empire.

Clay pipes, ivory lice comb, lead sounding weights and artifacts recovered from Spanish galleons.

"There were cannons and anchors about a hundred-fifty feet off the beach in ten feet of water. There were a lot of artifacts scattered over the whole fifty-five-acre site and beyond. We found a ten-and-a-half carat emerald ring, a Madonna with emeralds on the bottom of it. A gold chain, gold earrings, a boarding cutlass, pistols, silver plates, silver forks and spoons, lots of cannon and musket balls."

MEL FISHER'S ADMIRALTY CLAIMS

It was an era of discovery for Weller and the other divers he was working with. "In 1979, Mel Fisher came in and filed an admiralty claim on all the 1715 shipwreck sites not already under claim. That included five of the six and it included MacAllaster's site that we were working. Fisher literally arrested the sites with a federal officer on board," Weller said.

The only site Fisher could not claim was the *Urca de Lima* that Frank Allen, another treasure salvor, had already arrested in admiralty. "We had a standoff. MacAllaster had the state lease and Fisher had the admiralty claim. U.S. District Judge Mehrtens said everybody out of the water."

Nobody worked the shipwrecks during the summer season of 1980. Salvors typically could only work the inshore wrecks of the 1715 fleet in calm weather, which meant only during summer months. Mel Fisher and Richard MacAllaster used the time to work out a settlement.

"MacAllaster could salvage on the primary site of the fifty-five acres which in later years would become very lucrative. Fisher and MacAllaster went in front of U.S. District Court Judge James King with the proposal and the judge said: 'Make it happen.'"

The summer season of 1981 saw Weller and MacAllaster and their team of divers back in the water on the *Nieves* site. MacAllaster's salvage boat, *Bamboo Bay*, sank in a hurricane in 1979. It was refloated and was on the site along with *Pandion*, a twenty-four-foot salvage vessel owned and operated by John and Judy Halas. The *Nieves* site was worked until 1985.

"From 1981 to 1985 we had four good years. Recovered gold and silver every year. We were the only ones on the site. Harold Holden worked north of us in Mel Fisher's area. In 1985 MacAllaster decided to move off the site. Richard made the decision to pick up the five cannons and the pair of crossed anchors located between B and C markers."

ABOARD THE *WAG*

Margaret worked on friends' boats while Bob worked with MacAllaster during the time a "no women aboard" policy was in effect. MacAllaster eventually relented and accepted Margaret as a valued member of the salvage diving team.

"MacAllaster used his new thirty-foot salvage boat, the *WAG*, an acronym for Wild Assed Guess, to pick up the cannons. Margaret and I helped him pull up the cannons."

Margaret and Bob formed a unique and steadfast dive team and shared the excitement diving together on shipwrecks.

"The day the last cannon was picked up Margaret and I were on the bottom. We recovered silver forks and several pieces of eight. When a decision was made to pick up the two crossed anchors, I opted out." Bob shook his head.

The crossed anchors became symbolic. They were steadfast in an ocean of sand. When vandals would remove or destroy markers placed on the beach, divers could always reorient themselves by using the position of the two crossed anchors. The anchors became Weller's symbol for his own company, Crossed Anchors Salvage.

"If you raise 'em, you raise 'em yourself. I'd just assume you leave the anchors there," Weller told MacAllaster.

DEFIANCE

Margaret, Bob, and David Ward took the 32-foot salvage vessel *Defiance* and went to a site they called Jewelry Flats.

"I found a two-escudo gold coin under a beer can there with John Halas two years before. It was the farthest north that we ever found a gold coin."

The team speculated trying to determine where legendary beach-comber and treasure diver Kip Wagner found his horde of 1,500 gold coins in 1961. "It was up there somewhere so that's where I chose to work," Weller declared. They found two small silver coins that day.

On 14 July 1985, MacAllaster decided to pull up the two crossed anchors. He needed help raising them. Margaret volunteered to help him. Bob steadfastly refused. Those two crossed anchors, in his view, belonged

Swords, flintlock pistols, and cannonballs stabilized by electrolytic reduction recovered from sunken galleons.

where they were on the bottom. Bad enough MacAllaster pulled up the cannons.

Weller joined Whitey Keevan aboard Whitey's boat *Defiance*. Weller determined to look for the spot where Kip Wagner had found his horde of gold.

"We left the marina at 9 AM. The seas were calm, the water was clear. We had twenty-foot visibility, winds out of the southeast at five knots. We anchored nine-hundred feet offshore in eighteen feet of water," Weller said.

They anchored in front of the spot where beach marker C had been placed. MacAllaster had three beach markers denominated A, B, and C. They covered 1,800-feet of beachfront. His area extended 1,800-feet out into the ocean from the beach. The road to the beach came to A1A at A marker. It was about two-and-a-half miles south of the Fort Pierce Inlet.

THE GOLD ROSARY

"Whitey went in the water first. The depth of sand over Anastasia rock was six to eight feet. The rock base, once the sand was cleared away, was limestone. Whitey was down an hour. He came up with nothing. I headed for the bottom," Weller related.

"After about an hour swinging my metal detector, I got a hit and fanned up a .22 caliber bullet. People liked to shoot our buoys out there . . . and that's when the Moko Jumbies set in." The expression on Weller's face changed.

Moko Jumbies, to islanders and seafarers in the Caribbean, is a portend of powerful spirituality. Weller felt it at that moment.

"When I went down the water was calm. Suddenly *Defiance* began dragging its anchor." Bob was using a hookah regulator attached to the shipboard air compressor.

"I was being dragged along the bottom by my air hose. I was dragged about 75-feet before Whitey got the anchor hooked in. I found myself in a new spot on the bottom about 75-feet from where I'd started. I started working the metal detector and got another hit."

Weller supposed the second hit would be another .22 bullet. "I fanned down another foot-and-a-half. There was a gold medallion laying on the edge of the coral. We had started to blow but off to the side," he said.

The ship's mailbox blower was shooting the prop wash from the anchored boat down a metal elbow. The force of the water coming down dug holes in the sand that allowed divers below to see the bottom and get to limestone rock where artifacts settled.

"The more I dug the more gold started to show. I had three medallions with an interlocking gold chain. An angel with outstretched arms connected the three medallions."

The find was rare and extraordinary. The finely worked and delicate rosary measured 6½" x 8". Black ebony beads were connected by the gold chain.

"I continued to check the area and found a thimble and part of a block and tackle, then headed to the surface," Weller said.

Whitey Keevan leaned over the stern. Weller handed the rosary and artifacts up to him with the comment, "Whitey you are not going to believe this." Weller went back underwater to see if he could locate more of the rosary. He found nothing more so surfaced and gave Whitey a turn below.

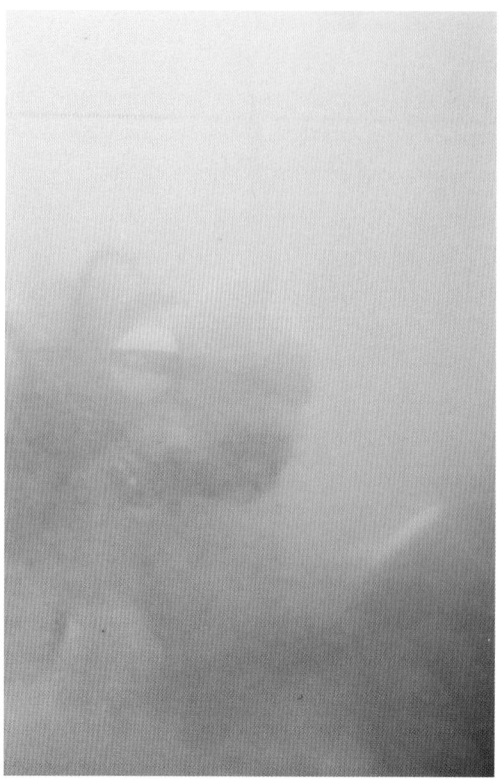

Bob Weller diving off Fort Pierce on a shipwreck site. Visibility near shore is very limited. Divers must often proceed by feel alone. The wide-angle underwater camera lens is within inches of Bob's head, yet it is difficult to make out his face and the metal detector he is holding.

"I'll put us into a box search. I know how to do a box search and there has to be more there," Weller told Keevan. Weller began blowing holes with the mailbox in methodical search patterns to cover the whole area below. "I got on the radio. MacAllaster had picked up the two crossed anchors and was already at the dock at Fort Pierce. I told MacAllaster that he ought to come out and see what we got and to bring Margaret with him."

Within fifteen minutes *WAG* was heading toward them. "Pretty soon MacAllaster came alongside, stepped aboard and I handed him the rosary. He said, 'That's pretty nice,' and popped it into a plastic bag and went back aboard *WAG*. Two other boats were working nearby, Harold Holden's boat and John Halas with Carl Ward aboard *Pandion*. They could see the commotion," Weller said.

Meanwhile Whitey Keevan was still working below. MacAllaster motored over to the Halas boat, showed them the rosary then went back to Fort Pierce dock.

"As *WAG* rounded the inlet, Whitey Keevan surfaced. He had a big grin on his face and had a six-foot gold chain in his hand. He'd found the rest of the rosary with its ebony beads."

It was 5 o'clock and Weller and Keevan decided to head back to the dock. "We had no written agreement. It was my site by this time. MacAllaster would get one third, I'd get two-thirds . . . the rosary hasn't been split yet." Weller interrupted his train of thought with recognition that after all this time Whitey Keevan still possessed the gold rosary and it had not been valued or shared out.

A BIG SURPRISE

"MacAllaster didn't know we'd found the rest of the chain. When we got in, MacAllaster said 'Let's do a roll on the girls.' I had a townhouse on Hernando Street. When we got there, I put a red velvet cloth on the table. MacAllaster laid out the rosary he had in the plastic bag and covered it with a towel," Bob related the incident.

Margaret had seen the rosary on the boat but Judy Halas and the other wives had not. MacAllaster went to gather up the wives and bring them to Weller's townhouse to unveil the cross.

"When MacAllaster was gone we added the chain to the cross and covered it over again with the towel. He got back and herded the girls into the front room and said, 'You are about to see something you have never seen before.' MacAllaster stepped to the table and lifted the towel. He was as shocked as anybody to see the complete rosary there." Weller beamed. Satisfaction showed in his eyes many years after the incident.

"MacAllaster said that he absolutely did not want any publicity about the find. It was the finest artifact found on the 1715 fleet that year but it received no publicity. A week to the day later Mel Fisher and his dive team found the *Atocha*. That overshadowed everything else and pushed the rosary into a corner."

WELLER BUYS *PANDION*

The agreement Weller worked out with MacAllaster had been hammered out one night after the cannons were raised. "When MacAllaster raised the cannons, he decided to quit the site. We had a mutual agreement that when he left, I would have exclusive salvage rights on the primary fifty-five acres. I bought John Halas' boat; a 24-foot trap boat fitted out for salvage called *Pandion*. We were ready to go."

Weller was ready but what had not been worked out with MacAllaster was the split if he found anything. "We had financial backers, an eager crew and we wanted at it. MacAllaster and I met at my townhouse in Fort Pierce to determine the split. This was a very memorable occasion." It amused him to think back fondly of the wrangling over deals with good friends.

"Knowing MacAllaster liked Michelob beer, I bought two six packs. We met at 7 PM. Mac sat facing me. While I nursed one bottle, he managed to consume the other eleven. We discussed the salvage, the length of the season and kept skirting around the split. What he should get and what I should get."

THE DEAL

"Finally, at 11 o'clock at night with MacAllaster hanging on to the table with one hand and only the desk lamp on, he looked across the table at me and said, 'Allright. What do you want?' I said seventy-five twenty-five."

View from the beach near location known as Kip's Cabin. It is here where legendary treasure-hunting pioneer Kip Wagner had his home. Working offshore is *Pandion* crewed by the Weller team.

"He said 'Sure, I'll give you twenty-five.' No, I said, it's the other way around. It costs a lot to keep a salvage operation going. Mac said, 'No way.' We finally agreed on two-thirds, one third. I would get two thirds in my favor." The deal made; Bob Weller used his company name Crossed Anchors Salvage.

"Those anchors were like friends. When MacAllaster picked them up off the bottom it was like losing friends," Weller lamented again. Weller imprinted the Crossed Anchor logo on books about treasure diving that he published.

"The first trip Margaret and I made out to the site on *Pandion* was at the end of July 1985. The water was turbid with three feet visibility.

It was windy. I dove first and was on the bottom. I couldn't see much. I came across what I thought was a chain laying across what seemed to be an oil pan welded to the bottom."

"I couldn't budge it so I left it and kept going. It wasn't until I dived on the *Atocha* and saw silver bars on the bottom that I realized I'd passed over a silver bar. It's still there. Somewhere on the bottom at the *Nieves* site there is a forty-pound silver bar."

Close view of some of the treasure recovered by the Wellers and their team.

Weller put together the A Team. The dive crew consisted of Bob Luyendyk, Steve Singer, Don Kree, Margaret, and himself.

"Each one of us knew what we were doing. How to cover the bottom, how to use a metal detector. We honed our skills through experience. There was still a lot of area that MacAllaster had not covered."

Other crewmembers were welcomed aboard *Pandion*. "George Hook found a nice five emerald gold ring with three amethysts. Don Kree found a gold ring. This established what we called Ringsville."

"One day I dropped into the area and picked up twelve gold rings. Bob Luyendyk picked up eight gold rings. We decided to work along the edge of the original beach."

"Where the beach had been in 1715 when the fleet wrecked and came ashore. The original beach was a hundred feet seaward of the present beach and covered by about eight feet of water. Luyendyk and I picked up a sixteen-inch diameter platter."

Diving alone the next day Weller discovered the edge of another silver platter. He surfaced, got his wife Margaret to put on her dive gear and join him below. Together they extracted the second sixteen-inch diameter platter.

"Steve Singer uncovered an encrusted bronze sword handle. He didn't know what it was and kept throwing it away. Don Kree would keep picking it up and putting it in front of him. Steve kept tossing it aside. After the third time, Kree pointed out the part of the bronze hilt. Steve could see it and he finally brought it up." Weller laughed. It was another amusing story that was told and retold by friends in their own manner years after the discovery was made.

Margaret and Bob dove together most of the time. "She could see the small coins I couldn't. When we dove together, Don Kree would position the boat topside and run the breathing compressor. On this particular dive, Don gave two pulls on the air hose. I responded yes with two pulls. Don moved the boat three feet."

"Just as we started moving, I got a hit. Whatever it was I didn't want it carried away by the blowers. I put my hand over it and hung onto a rock. Margaret saw it and gave me the signal underwater that it was a ring. For the next three minutes while Don was blowing, we held on like flags flying in the wind."

GOLD RINGS

When Don Kree finally shut down *Pandion*'s blower, Margaret and Bob both had their hands on top of the ring. "It had a floral design and a series of circles. The ring was 22.3 carats. All the rings were either coin gold, 22.3 high carat, or 12-carat low gold. Nothing much in between," Weller said.

Ringsville yielded seventy gold rings that first season to the divers of *Pandion*. Weller and his team continued working the *Nieves* site alone.

Bob and Margaret started a business they called Cabinet Man in 1982. They specialized in installing fine wooden cabinets. Bob's brother-in-law worked as an installer, Margaret was the secretary, their son Robbie was a salesman. They did more than a million dollars a year in retail sales.

"Cabinet Man gave us the opportunity to take a couple of months off in the summer. The business pretty much ran itself," Weller said. "We built townhouses on Hernando Street in Fort Pierce in 1982. We kept the model and sold the other three. We were on site. We could see the Fort Pierce Inlet and the ocean from our bedroom window. We could look out in the morning and if it was too rough to work, we would go back to sleep."

The townhouse turned into a diver's den. Divers would stay with Bob and Margaret. There were sleeping accommodations in a spare bedroom, a sleeping loft, and a sleeper downstairs in the living room.

Carl Ward, one of the veteran divers who worked the sites on and off with Bob over many years, commented that they formed the Gentlemen's Treasure Diving Association. Actually, with Margaret's amazing underwater treasure discoveries diving everyday with the team, the club wasn't exclusive to men only.

Bacon and eggs, hash brown potatoes, gourmet coffee for breakfast and the divers were ready to go. *Pandion* was five minutes from the townhouse docked at Inlet Marina.

WORKING THE 1715 WRECKS

"We would be on site by 8 or 9 o'clock. The trip from the marina to the *Nieves* site took twenty minutes. It was also called Colored Beach wreck site at one time. A throwback to segregation."

The first break in the weather for the 1987 summer season came in the second week in May. "We pinpointed an area in Ringsville about three hundred feet off the beach that we hadn't worked before. The year before, on the last week, we picked up two coins near that area."

"We anchored up by 8:30 AM and by 9:30 AM a boat came up from the south. It turned out to be *Pandion II*, four feet longer than our *Pandion*. On board were Craig Boyd and Coast Guard Ensign Richard Gilmore. They had permission from MacAllaster to work the site. It kind of shocked me when they dropped anchor only seventy-five feet off our own. That day they found two gold coins."

"We found nothing but silver. The next morning, we were on site by 8 o'clock. They were already sitting where we were the day before. My feeling was to dive someplace else. I chose an area two hundred feet further out on the reef where I had found a flintlock pistol and several pieces of a silver plate when I was diving with George Hook."

He went to the wall in his office where the original site chart made aboard *Pandion* was framed. "There is a row of holes. We blew fifteen holes in all. I said let's go to the end and continue the line of holes maybe we can pick up some more silver plate. We went out. Had a brand-new diver on board, Matt Hepler. Matt was a med student at Johns Hopkins University. He was down on vacation."

"Bob Luyendyk and Matt were the first ones down on the bottom. Bob Luyendyk told Matt before they jumped in that Matt was to move the stones while Bob worked the metal detector. When he found gold coins, Matt was to cup his hands and when they were full to bring them up to the surface. Matt was green and believed him and said OK. Visibility was good, twenty-five feet and the water was calm."

"The third hole was being blown when Hepler and Luyendyk surfaced. Hepler spit out his mouthpiece and asked, 'Is it gold?' Luyendyk nodded as he climbed on board."

A GOLD ROYAL

Weller held out his hand to receive the object while Luyendyk was still in the water. Luyendyk refused. He kept his hand clenched until he got into the boat. When he opened up his hand he held a Royal 8 escudo gold coin dated 1712.

Royals are rare coins. They were presentation pieces and were made to demonstrate the mint maker's skill. They were often sent to the King of Spain or other ranking officials.

"With MacAllaster we picked up seven Royals before so I knew what they were. We did a lot of jigging on the stern. Richard Gilmore could see us and knew something exciting was discovered. By 4 PM they pulled their anchor and came over."

The Hapsburg shield on a gold "Escudo." The Spanish word "Escudo" means shield.

"That was 1 July 1987. The next morning when we came out on site, Craig Boyd had *Pandion II* anchored where we had found the Royal the day before. We moved to where they had been working. We began picking up gold and silver."

It was during the previous winter of 1986 and 1987 that Margaret told the divers every chance she got that she was going to find a Royal. "Up to that point in time no woman diver had ever found a Royal and the chances were a million to one," Bob said.

THE STORY OF MARGARET'S ROYAL

"On 9 July 1987, we were anchored two-hundred feet off the beach, right where the old beach in 1715 was probably located. The bottom went out from the beach and dropped three feet. It had an eight-foot underwater slope but there it dropped abruptly." Frogfoot explained the underwater topography using his hands for emphasis.

"There were stumps of mangrove trees that had been worn down by waves so they were almost level with the bottom. One stump stood up about a foot off the bottom, right on the very edge of the former beach where it dropped off. That's where Margaret and I started to work that morning of July 9th."

Gold. Once you touch it, you never forget how it feels. Spanish mintage in the New World was renowned for its purity. In time, the Crown began to devalue its gold and silver content causing coins of later mintage to be of less value.

Bob began working a few feet north of the mangrove stump then switched to the south side. "Margaret held onto the stump and began fanning along the top at the edge of the drop off. Suddenly she was staring a Royal gold 4 escudo dated 1711," Bob related.

"Margaret put her hand on it, gasped and tried to grab me. I was just out of reach. Finally she was able to grab me and pull me over. When she lifted her hand I could see it was gold but didn't see it was a Royal. I started to pick it up. Margaret grabbed it and headed for the surface."

MARGARET TELLS THE STORY

"I decided to clear the sugar sand out of the stump. I was leaning way over the stump fanning sand away by hand when I got a glimpse of gold." Margaret Weller picked up the story and recounted her version of the tale.

"I thought it looked like a dinner plate. Bob Luyendyk had said when he found his Royal that it didn't seem real, that it was a diver's trick. I looked at the coin in the stump and the same thought ran through my mind. Bob Luyendyk is right, it does look fake," Margaret said.

"I tried to call Bob through my regulator. I had my hand on the coin. It had been there without moving for two-hundred-and-fifty years and it wasn't going anywhere. I kept my hand over it anyway," Margaret laughed.

"I couldn't reach him. Finally, I was able to pull Bob's fin. He came over. I raised my hand. We wore orange gloves at the time. I could see his big old, orange-gloved hand coming over to take my coin. I didn't want him to grab my coin so I grabbed it and went to the surface."

"The guys on board *Pandion* raised me over the dive platform. I yelled for them to get a camera. When I opened my hand here was this Royal four-escudo gold coin. The only picture that came out barely showed my hand with the gold coin in it," Margaret related.

EVERYBODY JUMPS IN

"One of the investors got so excited he took off my weight belt and took my regulator from me. I thought he was helping me aboard. No, he jumped into the water and went down. I couldn't go back in the water." Margaret laughed remembering the incident.

The investor was Eldridge Bravo. He had brought a wealthy friend of his along to enjoy a day on the ocean. He was too excited to wait on board so joined Bob below.

BOB BACK ON THE SURFACE

Bob surfaced to take a look at what Margaret had found. "Without getting out of the water I called up and said, 'Let me see your gold coin.' George Hook was aboard and he told me that I had to get aboard first. I didn't know it was a Royal. I went back down. Before I knew it Eldridge Bravo's buddy was also on the bottom."

When Bob surfaced and got aboard *Pandion*, he asked to see the coin. Margaret brought out a plastic bag with a tag on it. "I said 'But that's a Royal.' Margaret replied, 'Didn't you know?'"

A ROYAL CHAMPAGNE TOAST

"You toast a gold coin with champagne. We always keep it on ice. That night the investors took us to dinner and we toasted the Royal with champagne," Margaret smiled.

The salvage year produced a lot of treasures. The two Royals were auctioned off. The 8-escudo found by Bob Luyendyk and Matt Hepler brought $40,000 and the 4 escudo that Margaret found fetched $20,000. The team found a lot of rings as well as gold and silver coins.

6

THE *NIEVES* WRECK SITE

THE WELLERS AND THEIR DIVE TEAM, USING *PANDION*, WORKED on the *Nieves* site south of Sebastian, Florida, the next season. By this time, they had become legends in the treasure hunting community. Margaret's gourmet lunches packed aboard *Pandion* and the Weller hospitality and warmth drew divers to them to learn and work. Their fame was spreading.

"In 1988 we had Channel 5 television from West Palm Beach come aboard to do a story about us. I remember the TV cameraman's name was Cunningham. We were working in eighteen feet of water." Bob began another tale of adventure.

"While Cunningham filmed me on the bottom, I found a flintlock pistol. I pointed it at the camera as if I was shooting him. A short time later he was on top of the reef filming me, about fifteen feet away.

A seven-foot lemon shark swam between us. He filmed it with me in the background. That night we were on the news segment and the story line went something like, 'You are not going to believe what treasure divers go through.'"

THE GOLD CHAIN

The 1991 season was the year of the gold chain. Weller's recollection of the event is indelible. It is the tale of high seas adventure and discovery. The stuff dreams are made of.

"It was 22 June 1991. We fueled and by 8:25 AM we were heading out the inlet. There were three of us on board, Margaret, Bob Luyendyk and me." Bob's stories always began in an orderly, methodical way. Details were never omitted, minute details that drew his listeners into the story as though they were part of the adventure.

"It was flat calm and crystal clear. By 1991, John Brandon, another salvage diver, was working the site on subcontract to MacAllaster on a fifty-fifty basis. Back in 1979, John and Judy Halas recovered twenty-seven pieces of worked gold jewelry in a place we called the Jewelry Flats," Weller recounted.

"One was a big three-piece earring and a part of another three-piece earring with two of the pieces missing. The chart plotted the location of the find to within four feet of the edge of the reef where the water dropped off from twenty to twenty-six feet facing the beach."

"My intent that day was to find the other two pieces of that gold earring," Weller said. When Weller brought *Pandion* on site, John Brandon was anchored on the Jewelry Flats.

"Brandon's anchor lines were strung out like spider webs. He took up the whole reef with lines stretching three hundred feet. My initial reaction was to go elsewhere but I considered it and wanted to look for that earring. I pulled up and made the OK sign to John, he made the OK sign back and I dropped my bow anchor over his."

Weller reversed and positioned his two stern anchors, one out on each side of *Pandion*. They began to blow a hole on the edge of the reef. Weller took up the tale. "Bob Luyendyk was the first in the water. By 10:30 AM he was up and Margaret and I went down. We kept moving the boat toward the beach blowing holes. It was a flat sandy bottom so it went fairly quickly."

"By 1 o'clock Margaret and I were up to eat a sandwich and Luyendyk went down. He picked up a musket ball. By 3 o'clock Luyendyk was up and I went down by myself."

WIND PICKS UP

"By then the wind picked up to almost fifteen knots and the seas were two to four feet. The ship was bouncing pretty good." Weller worked underwater in good visibility.

"We were now about a hundred feet shoreward of the reef and it was 4 o'clock. Brandon decided he would go home. His diver Mike Maguire came over in the anchor boat to pick up Brandon's anchor. Our anchor buoy was wrapped up in his. With the wind and waves Maguire was having a tough time untangling it."

"Margaret called over and asked Maguire if he wanted to borrow a face mask. He came over to our boat, got it, but still had trouble untangling the lines. Brandon was impatient to get home."

"Margaret and Bob Luyendyk asked Maguire if he wanted them to give him slack with our bow anchor. He said it would help. As soon as Margaret and Bob Luyendyk let go our bow anchor line, with the wind and the waves, *Pandion* began drifting back toward the beach. I had no idea what was going on topside."

Bob Weller was using a hookah regulator attached to an air hose from the compressor aboard *Pandion*. As the boat was being pushed by wind and waves, Bob was being dragged along underwater. "I was dragged about seventy-five feet until Maguire got his anchor loose and Luyendyk took a turn on *Pandion*'s bow line to hold us and stop us drifting."

Margaret and Bob Luyendyk were not able to pull *Pandion* back to where they had been working. The wind and waves were now too strong. They hoped to continue where they left off so as not to interrupt the coverage of the bottom area but the boat had drifted.

Since they couldn't move the boat back to its original position, Margaret gave the air hose two tugs. That was a question directed to the diver below to ask if he wanted to dig.

"I pulled two back that meant dig the next hole. In the hole a nice pottery shard turned up. Topside Margaret and Bob said to each other, 'Let's dig one more hole and go home.' They tugged twice and I tugged back the go ahead signal," Weller said.

TREASURE FOUND

"The bottom was still flat. Suddenly while the hole was being dug I spotted this gold chain. It was all in a ball. I had the metal detector in one hand, the pottery shard in the other. I picked up the gold chain so I had my hands full. I had to surface," Bob explained.

He got to the stern of the boat. The seas now were three feet high. He had his hands full and he couldn't let go of anything. If he spit the regulator out of his mouth to call out he would get a mouthful of seawater. "All I could do was make muffled sounds through the regulator," Bob said. The exciting story that introduced this book now unfolded.

Margaret and Bob Luyendyk were in Pandion's wheelhouse facing forward. Margaret heard the muffled noise. Luyendyk told her he thought it was the ship's radio. Margaret thought it might be her husband so walked to the stern.

"Bob's got something," Margaret shouted to Luyendyk.

"She reached down and I handed her up the gold chain. Then I could grab hold of the boarding ladder. I said it's got to be at least three feet long. Margaret had marked the deck in one foot increments so they would know how much anchor line was let out," Weller recalled the incident.

Margaret unraveled the gold chain and stretched it out on the deck. "It's a lot longer than three feet," she commented. When accurately measured, the gold chain was eleven feet two inches long.

The team kept searching the same area where the gold chain was found until dark. The salvor's signal for a find that they wanted exclusive rights on was a red double buoy. Weller did not put up a red double buoy, rather placed a green buoy on the site and headed *Pandion* back to the dock.

They radioed the news and a lot of divers came down to the dock to see their find. It was a spectacular discovery.

Bob Weller was faced with two obstacles to his being able to keep the chain. The State of Florida could claim it as a unique artifact and the treasure had to be divided with MacAllaster.

"When James Levy, the Florida State Archaeologist, came up the following year to take photos for the division that year, I mentioned that I would like to keep the chain."

Levy told Weller that the state already had a gold chain and that he would not put it on the list of what the State wanted from that year's salvage.

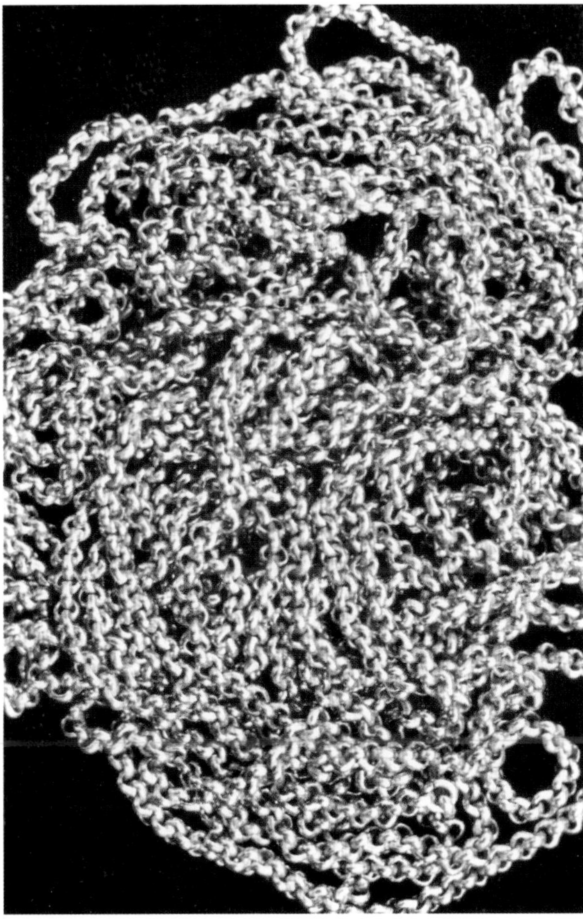

Gold chain recovered from a Spanish galleon site by the Weller team.

"It was quite a different matter with MacAllaster. We had a two thirds-one third split in my favor. The division took place in March 1992, in Matecumbe at Bernie Smith's place. Bernie was a friend of mine."

Weller knew what he wanted to give MacAllaster for his share of the gold chain. Mac's share of the value of the chain was about equivalent to eight gold two-escudo Bogota minted gold coins. Based on the going price for the two escudos, Weller drew cash out of his bank.

"A Bogota two-escudo coin was worth about two thousand bucks. I withdrew cash in hundred-dollar bills. I put the money in a briefcase and headed to Matecumbe for the meeting in the Keys. I stopped to get two six packs of beer. We waited at Bernie's for MacAllaster to show up."

WIRE CUTTERS

The meeting began at about 7:30 PM. MacAllaster's first words were, "We'll have no problem with the gold chain division. I brought wire cutters. We'll just cut one third for me and two thirds for you."

Weller's reply was rather direct. "If you touch that gold chain, I'll kick your butt. MacAllaster put away the better part of the two six packs of beer." The divers finally agreed that the whole gold chain was worth the equivalent of twenty gold two-escudo coins.

"I said I'll give you what seven gold escudos are worth in cash for your share of the chain and we'll call it square. I opened my briefcase and peeled off enough hundred-dollar bills to balance off seven escudos. That left $2000 in the briefcase in reserve. I closed the briefcase. MacAllaster saw that there was more money in the briefcase," Weller smiled.

"I pushed the pile of cash to him. He didn't pick it up. He said it's worth more than that. My question back was how much more than that?"

The back and forth went on for a moment. "How much money do you have left in that briefcase?" MacAllaster asked. Weller opened it and replied.

"Two thousand bucks. MacAllaster said he'd settle for that. I gave it to him and he settled for it. Both of us were happy." Bob and Margaret Weller kept the gold chain as a prized possession in their treasure collection.

The next year, 1992, was the last year that the Wellers worked the *Nieves* site. The last week of the season Weller put Bob Luyendyk in a fifteen by fifteen-foot area of Ringsville that they had not worked before. Within an hour Luyendyk found eight gold rings.

MacAllaster opened the *Nieves* site to any salvor who was willing to split with him fifty-fifty. "There were six boats all blowing deep holes. We decided not to go back."

7

THE QUEEN'S JEWELS

THE 1993 TREASURE DIVING SEASON ARRIVED. WELLER AND HIS team decided to work as sub-contractors with Mel Fisher on 1715 shipwreck sites. Fisher had admiralty claims on most of the areas where the 1715 fleet went down from Fort Pierce to Sebastian.

By May 1993, Weller moved *Pandion* to Sembler's Marina at Sebastian. Mel Fisher offered contracts on the various sites for $1,000 plus an agreement that subcontractors would split fifty-fifty with him after the State took a 20 percent share off the top for the privilege of leasing the sites in state territorial waters.

NEW LAW

The law of salvage is complex. Before passage of federal legislation in Chapter 39 under Title 43 of the Public Lands Act, sunken shipwrecks could be arrested by salvors in admiralty. This was the federal law of finds and claims. Salvage law gave the federal courts jurisdiction to establish claim and ownership of sunken vessels. The Abandoned Shipwreck Act changed all that. While many states already had artifact protection laws in so far as shipwrecks were concerned, state jurisdiction in navigable waters was superseded by federal admiralty.

A ground swell mounted by state officials and concerned professional archaeologists saw the eventual passage of the hotly contested federal law by Congress in 1988. The Abandoned Shipwreck Act, effective on April 28, 1988, added maritime areas to laws like the federal Archaeological Resources Protection Act and the National Historic Preservation Act.

Mel Fisher's admiralty claims, filed prior to the passage of the Abandoned Shipwreck Act, were "grandfathered" in.

Despite Fisher's rights under his preexisting admiralty claims, the group worked out a deal with the State of Florida to let the state take artifacts of historical or archaeological importance and share 20 percent of what was found.

Weller, for his group of investors and divers, signed a contract with Fisher in 1993 to work Corrigan's wreck site off Sebastian Beach with the proviso that they would receive half of what was left after the state took its share.

"It was seven miles from Sebastian to Corrigan's wreck site. We were three miles from the inlet. It took us about an hour to make the ten-mile trip," Weller said. The return trip in late afternoon took longer since the Atlantic Ocean would get rough later in the day. A sandbar at the mouth of Sebastian Inlet shifted and made passage through difficult at times.

CABIN WRECK SITE

"We passed the Cabin Wreck every day. There were boats working the Cabin wreck site. The Cabin site was the shipwreck of the *San Roman*, *Almirante* of the 1715 fleet. Corrigan's is the *Capitana* of the fleet, the *Regala*," Bob explained.

The Cabin wreck site got its name from the fact that Kip Wagner, one of the original treasure salvors of the 1715 fleet, had his beachfront cabin on the spot. "If Kip's cabin had been there in 1715, the *Almirante* would have gone right in his front door," Weller said. "Corrigan's is about five miles south of the Cabin wreck. Where the *Capitana* sank, Hugh Corrigan owned that whole stretch of beach. Hugh picked up all kinds of gold and silver off the beach and never told anybody."

The *San Roman*, *Almirante* of the 1715 Fleet, the ship that normally was heavily armed and carried the admiral of the convoy aboard and would provide rear guard for the plate fleet, was armed with fifty-four cannons.

"We found 28 of the cannons scattered over a three- to four-mile area of the bottom. After May and June, we figured that our divers and boat were being beat up by the long trip from the dock to Corrigan's wreck site. We decided to work the Cabin site. The trip was shorter and it would give us more bottom time."

Weller was advised by Roy Volker, one of the veteran salvage divers working with Fisher, to discuss his plans with John Brandon. Brandon had rights to work an exclusive area directly in front of Kip Wagner's cabin.

"We agreed on a handshake," Weller smiled. His team got a six-hundred-foot diameter area around the primary Cabin site. In the center was the cannon area where Kip had found most of his gold and silver in the sixties. Brandon would get 10 percent of what was found by the Weller group.

"We went to work 1 July 1993. I put four buoys out in the area I wanted to work. We anchored *Pandion* near the northeast buoy that was on the top of the first reef. We started blowing."

"One of our divers, a man who had just signed on that season, liked to bird dog. Take a tank and go off with a metal detector away from the anchored boat. His name was Chris James."

On this day Chris put on a tank, took a metal detector, and jumped over side to see what he could find. "Chris got easily seasick on the boat. It was always better to get him in the water," Weller said.

"I was on the bottom at about 10 o'clock. I found some pottery shards and the neck of an olive jar. I got four pulls on my air hose. That meant get your butt up to the boat quick."

"When I got to the stern of the *Pandion*, Chris James was in the boat all out of breath. He explained that he had found a 'gold thing full of stones' but had lost it and he was out of air. He had a hole in the bag he carried and the object dropped out."

"While I was putting another tank on him, Chris James made the comment, 'You don't think I was dreaming, do you?' I told him, no, he found something and I'd help him find it again." The diver got back in the water. Weller remained aboard *Pandion* and pulled it toward a marker buoy about twenty-five feet from the boat where the diver said he'd found the object.

GOLD BROOCH AND JEWELRY

"Just as Margaret, Bill Cassinelli and I brought *Pandion* over to the buoy, Chris popped to the surface waving a gold brooch, hollering, 'I found it.' It turned out the brooch had diamonds in it."

Weller went over the side. "I just got to the bottom and had started working when he came over to me and handed me this round gold brooch. We later counted 177 blue, white diamonds in it."

"Chris James had eyes as big as saucers. I brought the brooch to the surface and handed it to Margaret, who commented 'I wonder what is going to come up next.'"

Bob returned underwater. The depth was about twelve feet. The reef about two-and-a-half feet high and about four- to five feet long.

"CJ was working one end of the reef and I started working the other. Within minutes I got a hit with my metal detector and recovered a gold pineapple shaped earring. I showed it to Chris James then took it to the surface. That earring turned out to have 54 diamonds in it." Excitement and energy charged his voice.

There is a thrilling moment when treasure is brought up from a shipwreck. Who held the artifact in those final moments before the ship was lashed by wind and waves into its final resting place underwater? Objects recovered from the deep make history come alive.

"Margaret got on the phone to Bob Luyendyk who worked as a Project Engineer with Perry, the submersible builders in Riviera Beach. She told him we were into something and to take the next day off. He turned up the next morning at 6 AM."

"The next day our son Alan also came up so we had Chris James, Bill Cassinelli, Bob Luyendyk, Margaret, Alan and I aboard *Pandion*. We found the gold jewelry a hundred-fifty feet north of Kip's cabin up against the shoreward side of the first reef. The water was twelve feet deep but only four feet above the reef. There was a sandy bottom between the beach and the reef."

TREASURE BONANZA

"We picked up 22 gold rings, a silver candelabra, silver buckles, and a triangular piece of jewelry called a lazo that had 17 blue white diamonds in it. Bob Luyendyk found the second earring about fifteen feet from where I found the first one." "We found two gold toothpicks and a gold fingernail set.

By noon we located two anchors fifteen feet from the edge of the reef. The anchors were sitting upright on the bottom, flukes straight up in the air." Weller motioned with his hands, palms parallel, hands spaced close together.

"They had been carried as spares since we found them side by side. One was ten-feet long the other fourteen-feet. It was under the flukes of the fourteen foot anchor that we found the silver candelabra."

AMAZING FINDS

The diamond-studded gold jewelry has been dubbed the Queen's Jewels by Weller and his team of divers. The gold is 22.3 carat and the diamonds have a blue, white cast. The finds were among the most extraordinary ever recovered from a sunken ship. They were put on display at the Fisher treasure museum in Sebastian, Florida. When the Queen's Jewels were sold in 2009, they brought $850,000.

"By the time we got back to our townhouse in Sebastian, it was dark. The banks were closed. We couldn't leave the treasure in our unoccupied townhouse so each day we packed the Queen's Jewels into our cooler and

Close-up of brooch from the Queen's Jewels. The stone in the middle was never found.

Close-up of a pair of earrings found underwater, part of the "Queen's Jewels." Each earring was found quite a long distance from the other, a miracle of modern underwater detector technology and meticulous searching by the Weller team.

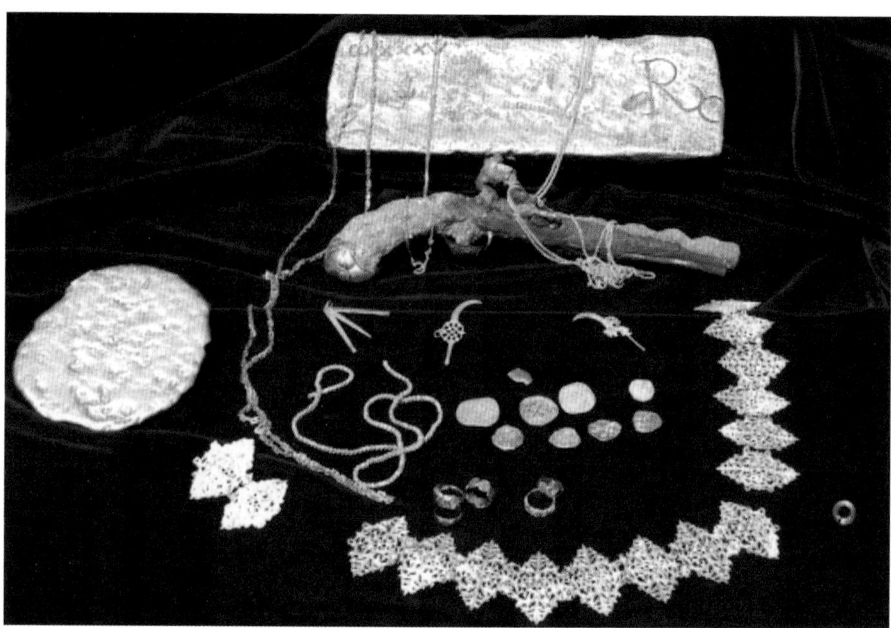

Sunken treasure. The stuff dreams are made of. A heavy silver bar, a gold splash weighing 9.4 pounds, a flintlock pistol, coins and gold chains, belts, and rings.

Diver Chris James with his Garrett underwater metal detector. Chris found the first piece of jewelry from what was to be called the "Queen's Jewels." Bob Weller's back is to the camera as he adjusts *Pandion*'s mooring anchor.

put our lunch on top of it then went back to the site," Weller laughed. He shook his head considering the chance they took with a fortune of booty from the sunken galleon.

SITTING ON THE BOOTY

"One day Kane Fisher came over to our site. Kane, one of Mel's sons, had a reputation for barging in where other salvors were working after they had been finding treasure. Kane stepped aboard *Pandion* and sat on the cooler. He asked if we had been finding anything. I said, no, just pottery shards," Weller grinned. Up to this point they had told no one about the Queen's Jewels.

"On July 7th a quick storm out of the southwest caught us by surprise. The wind was thirty knots and the seas built to six feet. Our boat was anchored within a few feet of the reef. There was an absolute chance we could have hit the reef and sunk. We had to de-anchor fast and get out of there," Weller said.

Airlift in use underwater.

Divers Chris James, Bob Weller, Margaret Weller, and John Christopher Fine (no shirt) holding the "Queen's Jewels."

Recollection of the peril *Pandion* was in with all the treasure they had found at the Cabin site in the lunch cooler brought back the excitement they shared aboard that day. "We had pretty much looked over the area."

"We decided to make an announcement and turn the treasure in. We didn't want it to end up back on the reef. We picked July 9th as the day we would announce our finds. Chris James' stepfather had media contacts and arranged television coverage. That day, when we came back to Sembler's Marina, the dock was crowded with forty people, TV and newspaper reporters."

Bob was on NBC television news. The story was in all the papers. The Fisher's made a big display of the gold jewelry in their museum in Sebastian.

Weller's team of treasure divers and investors had a terrific season. They recovered a total of 2,700 artifacts.

8
THE CABIN WRECK SITE

THE WELLER TEAM WORKED THE CABIN WRECK SITE, LOCATED in front of and near Kip Wagner's original house on the beach, for two more summer seasons in 1994 and 1995. They raised $130,000 from investors based on their success in 1993.

"We planned on expanding the salvage program on the Cabin site to concentrate on a shallow area between the beach and the first reef," Weller explained.

The area from the beach at the Cabin site consisted of a "Coral reef that you walked out on. It is a reef with sand on top of it. Then it drops six feet and the first reef seaward is 75 to 100 feet from shore."

"That first reef was full of holes. We called them monkey holes. They were covered with sand. The water was only two feet on top of that reef so we couldn't get *Pandion* in there."

"In 1994 our project was to buy jet boats with a very shallow draft. We would rig them with a novel blowing system and see if we could work the shallow area near the beach. They were picking up coins on the beach after every hurricane."

Bob contacted Regal, a jet boat manufacturer in Orlando. They were willing to discount the jet boats in exchange for publicity treasure finds would generate.

"A fourteen-foot jet boat listed for a little over ten thousand. They agreed to sell us two of them for eight thousand apiece if we would mention them in publicity."

Weller signed a contract and while the two new jet boats were being built, they purchased two more used fifteen-foot jet boats for $3,500 each.

"What I had in mind was to attach an irrigation hose to the boat's jet blower that could be manually put on and taken off easily. I also wanted to be able to attach a twenty-five-foot two-inch diameter fire hose to the blower. That extended our blowing capabilities to shallow water."

The winter saw the salvors getting the boats ready and equipped with anchors, mooring lines, and hookah gear. The operation was equipped and ready to go by May 1, 1994.

"We put the boats in the water. I put Gordon McCann in charge of one of the new boats. I took another jet boat around and parked it on the Intracoastal Waterway behind the other side of Kip's Cabin."

"We were standing on the porch of Kip's Cabin the first day of operations. Pete Fallon and myself. Pete had bought the original Kip Wagner cabin. We were on the porch talking. I saw that Gordon McCann's boat was in trouble." Weller shook his head; dismay crossed his face. It was also a look of consternation as he recalled the incident.

CAPSIZED

"The seas were four feet high. Gordon and his diver had gotten too close to the beach and they couldn't get the jet boat off. Suddenly as we were watching from the porch the jet boat turned over." Weller looked vexed. He shook his head again as he recalled the sinking of one of the new jet boats.

"George Hook and I left Kip's cabin and jumped onto our jet boat to help Gordon and his diver. It was a two-mile run to the Sebastian Inlet from where we were on the Intracoastal, then a two-mile run down the ocean to get to them. By the time we reached them the jet boat was completely underwater and was filling with sand as the waves battered it."

Margaret brought *Pandion* around and the divers put the sunken jet boat in tow. They were able to tow it through Sebastian Inlet and get it to a boat ramp then trailer it to a house they were renting.

"George Hook took the engine apart to get the salt water out. It turned out to be a nine-day job to strip the engine down. The boat suffered a lot of damage. It was a brand-new fiberglass boat. We took it back to the factory. They charged us $2500 to bring the boat back to good condition."

JET BOATS CONTINUE TO WORK NEAR SHORE

The other jet boats and *Pandion* continued working. The jet boats only required eight inches of water to work so the divers were able to blow sand away in the very shallow inshore areas.

"We got in close to the beach and blew a lot of sand away. One of the nicest pieces of eight that we found was right in shallow water. In that 1994 season we found some pieces of gold chain out on the third reef with *Pandion*. One of the divers, Jimmy Smith, found the gold cross that went with the gold chain working two hundred feet further away."

A jet boat is powered by water that is blown out a hole in the stern. A flapper covers the hole. Weller used his engineering skills and designed a pin system to raise the flapper, insert a metal rod to hold it out of the way then used an irrigation pipe that was clamped onto the outlet of the jet. The irrigation pipe could be bent at any desired angle to direct the stream of water coming out of the jet. Ninety degrees enabled the divers to blow a hole straight down, 45 degrees enabled them to dig at a slant.

Weller designed fittings so that a fire hose could be rigged at the jet's outlet. Divers could use the fire hose to blow sand away from an underwater work site even in areas where the jet boat could not be anchored.

"The jet boats blew sand like you wouldn't believe. One time we put two jet boats together and blew down six feet. They were a great innovation for working in shallow. They could be used in eight inches of water."

It had to be flat calm for the jet boats to work. Waves and wind would bounce the jet boats on sharp coral reefs. It happened so frequently that the Weller team spent a lot of time re-fiber glassing the bottoms. In one area the divers found several one- and two reals that had legible dates from the mints in Lima and Mexico City.

Broken pieces of K'ang Hsi porcelain came up in an area close to the beach. The excitement from finds made the previous season generated a lot of interest in Weller's inshore project. Ken and Christine Potter, a couple from Pennsylvania, worked the full season and operated one of the jet boats.

K'ang Hsi porcelain cup recovered intact from Spanish galleon. Fine Chinese porcelains were brought across the Pacific by Spain's Manila galleons. The cargoes were taken by mule across Mexico from the Pacific port of Acapulco to Vera Cruz then put aboard ships heading back to Spain.

Don Cook, owner of Don Cook Auto Sales in West Palm Beach, rented a house right on the beach in front of where the jet boats were working. Don ran another of the jet boats.

The Wellers rented a house on a canal where they could dock *Pandion* during the 1995 and 1996 season. "The house was supplied with well water and it smelled bad," Bob recalled.

After a day of work the dive team would jump into the swimming pool instead of taking a shower. The team consisted of as many as fourteen divers at a time. "It was not unusual for us to have fourteen people for dinner. We were three miles from the Sebastian Inlet which required a trip north up the Intracoastal Waterway to get to the inlet for access to the Atlantic."

MO MOLINAR

Interest piqued when veteran diver Mo Molinar, one of Mel Fisher's original divers, who worked the *Atocha* and *Santa Margarita* sites off Key West, moved his salvage vessel, *Virgalona,* some 300 feet north of the McLarty Museum. The museum was built right on the beachfront in Vero Beach and houses artifacts from the 1715 Fleet. Mo anchored *Virgalona* between the beach and the first reef.

"Mo picked up two gold rosaries, two gold buckles, ten gold rings, and ten cloak buttons in a twelve-foot-deep area of the first reef just seventy-five feet off the beach. Mo's discoveries started a parade of salvagers into the Cabin wreck site. By 1994, there were eight or nine boats there all the time."

Weller and his team continued to work the near shore area in front of Kip's cabin.

"Directly in front of Kip's cabin, the seaward side of the first reef is really gouged where a Spanish galleon hit. In the gouge Margaret and I picked up an adz with a handle on it and bark on the handle along with a lot of small coins."

"Just over the top on the shoreward side of that reef lay eleven cannons that the *San Roman* dropped on its way into the beach. Directly in front of Kip's cabin in eight feet of water and two hundred feet north in front of the Smith residence, right up against the reef is another nine foot cannon."

Bill Cassinelli (eyeglasses) with Hank Haart in the McLarty Museum near the site where the 1715 Spanish treasure fleet wrecked. The divers are viewing artifacts recovered from sunken ships in that fleet.

During the 1994 and 1995 seasons, the Wellers concentrated the salvage effort in front of Kip's cabin where a major section of the *San Roman* came apart. It was an area that Kip Wagner's original group of salvors had covered pretty well.

"They missed the Queen's Jewels," Weller reminded people skeptical of working where other salvors had been before them. The Weller team found an intact harquebus gun, several hundred coins, gilded chess pieces, silver buckles, and a silver cloak button.

Despite the fact that they were recovering coins and artifacts, the number of salvage boats that moved onto the Cabin wreck site caused their decision to return to the Corrigan wreck site for the 1996 through 1999 seasons. The divers recovered more coins and pottery shards but nothing like the finds they had made in 1993 on the Cabin site.

Mo, like so many underwater explorers and pioneers, passed over the bar. His legend finding gold lives on everywhere tales of sunken treasure are told.

9

THE QUEST FOR THE GREATEST UNRECOVERED TREASURE IN THE WORLD

IN 1997 WELLER BOUGHT A 37-FOOT STRIKER, ALUMINUM HULLED vessel. He outfitted it for long-range salvage and dubbed it *Expedition*. He had an idea in mind that had intrigued him for many years.

"In 1997, Ernie Richards and I took over publication of *Treasure Quest Magazine*. It was a full-time job. A lot of people wrote stories for us and we had fun," Weller said. It was a roundabout tale but would eventually lead back to the Striker and his search for a fabled Spanish galleon.

"Ernie Richards had worked for Perry Oceanographic as an electrical engineer. Ed Schroeder was the publisher of *Treasure Quest*. Ed had put out the magazine on his own for a long time. I had been writing articles for Ed over many years so the readers knew who I was."

"Ed had a baby born with a hole in its heart. As a result, Ed and his wife Debbie spent the next three months in the hospital with their baby daughter. The magazine was not being published. Some of the readers were calling me and asked why they were not receiving the magazine."

The story took another detour as Bob described a Halloween trip he and Margaret along with Ernie Richards and his wife Ellie had made

A splash of silver. Untaxed and unstamped contraband recovered from a Spanish galleon. The illegal practice of smuggling gold and silver to avoid paying the Royal Fifth, a 20 percent tax to the Crown, was widespread in colonial times.

to Cancun, Mexico in the winter of 1996. "It was on that vacation that I mentioned to Ernie the idea of publishing *Treasure Quest Magazine* ourselves. Ernie agreed."

THE SAN JOSE

"The *San Jose* project started with one phone call." The story was coming out slowly, a little suspense, a little wait, a couple of detours while Weller set the stage, then directly into the tale of his search for the fabled Spanish treasure galleon sunk off Cartagena Harbor in 1708 by English warships.

Treasure Quest Magazine exposed Bob "Frogfoot" Weller's byline to the salvage community. When he and Ernie Richards took it over, they opened an office in a commercial complex in West Palm Beach. The office became a gathering place for salvors passing through Florida.

This eclectic group of adventurers all had tales to tell. The magazine gave their efforts legitimacy. They either became published authors themselves or Ernie and Bob reported on their projects.

While Weller's name was not as well known to the general public as legendary Mel Fisher, his fabulous discoveries over four decades working Florida treasure sites and exposure through *Treasure Quest*, began to draw other salvors to him.

"I didn't know him. I never heard from the man before. Dr. Daniel Navaez is a geologist. He studied at the University of Colorado but is a resident of Bogota, Colombia. Daniel's family dates back to when Cortez was exploring Mexico. Navaez is mentioned in Cortez' memoirs."

"Daniel was president of a large emerald mine in Colombia. The Colombian government contracted with him to explore the Seranilla Banks off the coast to determine if something of mineralogical value was there that the government could take advantage of."

"While Daniel Navaez was scouting the area, he stumbled onto a forty-two cannon wreck site in the water. He had his secretary do a search in the Bogota library to see what she could find out about shipwrecks," Weller explained.

Dr. Navaez' secretary found reference to the 1604 sinking of Admiral DeCordoba's fleet that may have sunk on the Seranilla Banks. The ships were loaded with gold and silver. "Enough so that Daniel quickly became involved with shipwreck salvage."

"Hence the phone call." Daniel Navaez had some of Weller's published books on shipwrecks along the Florida coast as well as copies of *Treasure Quest Magazine*. He wanted to talk.

"I invited him to our house. Daniel had a condo in Boca Raton which was pretty close. The next day he knocked on my front door. We sat down in my gazebo on the water and started discussing shipwrecks on the Seranilla Banks."

As the men got to know each other, Weller described his interest in the wreck of the *San Jose*. Weller kept files and research notes, charts, archive documents, and copies of translations of ship's logs in his office. He had begun researching the *San Jose* some six years earlier.

"The *San Jose* is the richest un-recovered treasure, either land or sea, in the world. I estimate the value of its cargo to be as high as $4 billion," he said.

The *San Jose* lay on the bottom less than five miles off the Colombian coast. "The more we discussed the *San Jose*, the more Daniel was interested. Daniel asked me, 'Why don't you get a lease on the *San Jose*?' I replied, 'I would if I could.'"

Navaez then told Weller that his friend and schoolmate Andres Pastrana was to be inducted as President of Colombia in September 1997. "Navaez said he could get me a lease. We decided to form a corporation. His lawyer would draw up the paperwork. That got it rolling."

Weller had offers of financial backing. A longtime friend from his Honeywell days, Jim MacDonald, joined the project. Jim moved into Weller's spare bedroom and the men planned as they put together a *San Jose* prospectus for investors.

CARTAGENA OFFSHORE

The next step was for Weller and his fledgling team to visit Cartagena and explore the site. "In 1998, Jim MacDonald, myself and an employee of Dr. Navaez rented a boat and took a trip to the area around Isla de Tesoro. Treasure Island."

The imposing fort at the entrance to Cartagena's harbor offered protection to ships that could make it inside.

The fort at the entrance to Cartagena harbor protected the city from attack and shielded ships that made it in safely.

An Indian sculpture adorns the preserved fort in Cartagena.

The Cartagena Gold Museum exhibits native gold jewelry and adornments.

Gold, the lure that brought conquest. Quest for gold and human greed resulted in destruction of native cultures and enslavement of the people.

Native peoples used gold as ornaments. Rare examples of gold jewelry are displayed in Cartagena's Gold Museum.

The men stopped at Navaez' lawyer's oceanfront home on a neighboring island, Isla Grande. It was a seven bedroom, four bath home that the lawyer used only in the summertime. He offered the home to the salvors to use during the project.

Weller felt he was making good progress. They made inquiry about costs: fuel, dockage, weather conditions. They obtained local charts.

"The key to this thing was that I had been an active naval officer. I knew what the admiral had in mind in 1708, when he was bringing his Spanish treasure fleet into Cartagena Harbor from Porto Bello."

There were ample records as a result of the Spanish investigation after the battle that saw several of their ships sunk including the treasure galleon *San Jose*. Weller obtained logs from the English ships that took part in the battle.

THE 1708 SPANISH FLEET

The Spanish 1708 Fleet was in Porto Bello Harbor in Panama when a Swedish ship came into port. The captain reported that British warships were cruising off Cartagena. The Spanish commander General Don Joseph Santillan called the fleet's admiral Don Miguel Agustin de Villanueva to a meeting with all of the ship's captains and the merchants. The merchants had valuable cargo aboard destined for Spain, therefore had a vested interest in the safety of the fleet.

"The overall opinion of the captains and merchants was to wait until the English warships left the area. General Santillan and Admiral Villanueva decided to leave Porto Bello despite British presence off Cartagena. They downplayed the British threat. Admiral Villanueva made the comment, 'The seas are wide and its courses diverse,'" Weller explained.

The Spanish fleet consisted of some fourteen ships. When sighted by the British, Commodore Wager reported "Seventeen sails." French merchant ships were among them.

There are three major islands off Cartagena. They are called Baru or Brue islands by the English. Named Isla Rosario, Isla Grande, and Isla Tesoro by the Spanish.

When the Spanish fleet came up against Isla Grande the wind was against them. Admiral Villanueva had the fleet off Isla Grande and dropped their sails. The Spanish decided to wait until daylight to enter Cartagena Harbor.

"They thought that the heat of the mainland would cause air to rise and create an onshore breeze to carry them into the harbor. Once at the harbor mouth a Spanish fort could protect them as they made for Boca Chica cut."

The onshore breeze did not materialize as the Spanish expected. They raised sail in the morning and proceeded past Isla Grande around Isla Tesoro. The distance was six miles around Isla Tesoro then through Boca Chica pass into Cartagena Harbor.

"The English were to the east. They saw the Spanish around noontime on 8 June 1708. The British saw the masts of the Spanish ships. That told them they were about twelve miles away. What wind there was, was in favor of the British who headed to intercept the Spanish fleet."

THE BATTLE

Weller's description of the battle followed: "The Spanish saw 'em comin.' Right up until 5 o'clock Admiral Villanueva thought he could make the turnaround Isla Tesoro. At 5 o'clock the Spanish admiral saw they could not make it around the island. He sent flags up to signal form a line of battle."

The Spanish ships were within a half-mile of each other in a line with the larger armed ships facing the British. The Spanish were supported by armed *pataches* to the rear of the line.

"The British closed and the battle began a little before dark. At about 6:45 PM the British warship *Kingston* closed on the *Almirante* of the fleet, the *San Joaquin*, first in the Spanish line. The Spanish *Capitana* was the *San Jose*, it was next in line. Then the Vice-Admiral's ship *Santa Cruz*, also called the *Gobierno* was next. The *Urca de Nietto* was between the *Capitana* and the *Gobierno*." Weller used a hand-drawn chart to describe the battle plan.

The English warships consisted of the *Kingston*, *Portland*, *Expedition*, and a fire ship called the *Vulture*. The *Vulture* was only to be used to set enemy vessels on fire, it was not part of the battle.

"The *Kingston* engaged the *Almirante* in a fire fight. It was thirty minutes before the *Expedition* could get into position to fire on the next ship in line, the *San Jose*. The *Expedition* and the *San Jose* began their exchange of broadsides after dark. It was about 7:15 PM."

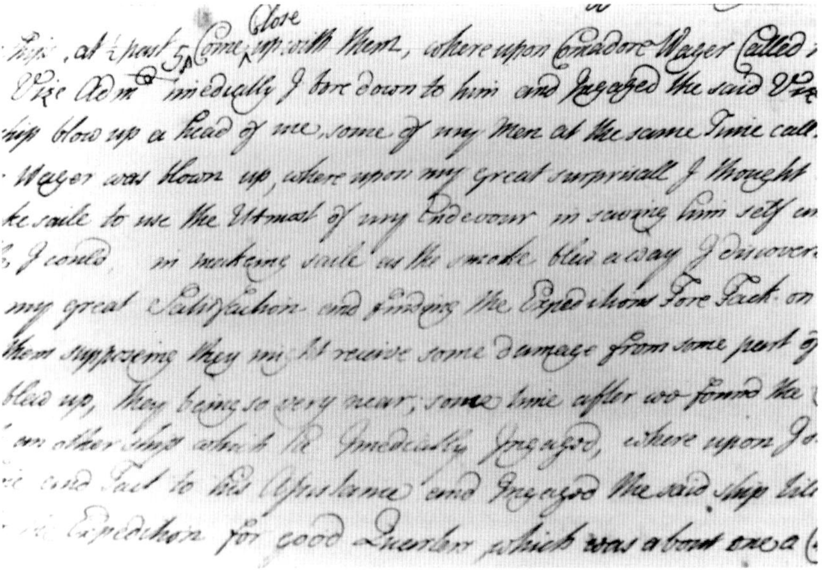
at ½ past 5 Close Come up with them, where upon Comadore Wager Called
Vice Adm^ll imediately I bore down to him and Ingaged the said V
ship blow up a head of me, some of my Men at the same Time call
Wager was blown up, where upon my great surprisall I thought
to use the Utmost of my Endeavour in saving him self or
I could in making saile as the smoke blew away I discover
my great Satisfaction and finding the Expedition Fore Sail on
them supposing they might receive some damage from some part of
blew up, they being so very near; some time after we found the
an other ship which he Imediately Ingaged, where upon I
said Sail to his Assistance and Ingaged the said ship
Expedition for good Quarter which was about one a

Log of Admiral Wager's flagship describing the attack on *San Jose*.

"The captain of the *Portland* never had a stomach for the fight. His ship was way behind and he did not take part in the battle. After the third exchange of broadsides a cannon shot from the *Expedition* hit *San Jose*'s magazine and the *San Jose* blew out her sides and sank quickly."

"Flaming wood hit the *Expedition*. Waves caused by the explosion almost came into *Expedition*'s lower gun ports. That's how close they were. When the smoke cleared after about fifteen minutes, the *San Jose* was gone. The *Expedition* picked up eleven survivors."

Commodore Charles Wager won the battle but lost a treasure-laden galleon to the bottom of the sea. The Spanish ships headed away around the island for protection. Commodore Wager aboard *Expedition* saw the silhouette of a ship ahead. He maneuvered *Expedition* in the darkness.

"By midnight the *Expedition* came upon the stern of Captain Conde de Vega de Floride's *Gobierno Santa Cruz*. Commodore Wager's first broadside took out the stern. The *Expedition* began circling the Spanish ship pouring broadsides into her. The *Kingston* had already broken off its engagement with the *Almirante*. The *Kingston*'s captain saw the explosion and thought it was *Expedition*. He went to pick up survivors."

"The *Kingston* joined the *Expedition* and now they were joined by *Portland*. The English poured broadsides into the Spanish ship. By 2 AM half the Spanish guns were destroyed and many seamen were wounded or killed."

"About this time, out of the darkness, sailed the Spanish *Almirante*. It came so close to Commodore Wager's *Expedition* that it almost brushed its side. It put a full broadside into the *Expedition* as it passed."

The *Almirante* passed on in the night headed for Boca Chica pass into Cartagena Harbor. It was too late to save the *Gobierno*. The *Almirante* saved itself and the treasure it had loaded aboard. The *Gobierno* had no treasure.

"The *Gobierno* fired two shots from the stern that signaled surrender. That was the end of the battle. The next day the British spotted the *Almirante* becalmed outside Boca Chica pass into Cartagena harbor. Commodore Wager sent *Portland* and *Kingston* after the *Almirante*."

"The *Kingston* fired on the *Almirante* but did no damage. The pilot told the captain that the *Kingston* was close aboard the reef at Salmedina and would not take responsibility. Thus, the *Kingston* and *Portland* turned back to help Commodore Wager with the captured ship."

"The captains of the *Portland* and *Kingston* were both court martialed for failing to take decisive action. Both lost command of their ships."

"Both as a navy officer and a salvager I believe I know where the *San Jose* went down."

"Daniel and I applied for a 38 square mile lease in the potential area. I could have narrowed that down to three square miles and still have found the *San Jose*."

GETTING READY FOR SEARCH AND SALVAGE

When he returned to the United States from his scouting trip to Colombia, Weller and his team began training. They purchased an Edgetech Model 1000 side scan sonar for $60,000. They fitted out the Striker with a fathometer that could profile the bottom showing a fifty-foot area in five hundred foot depths if required. Radar and an autopilot were installed on the *Expedition*, along with two computers.

The salvage boat was named for Commodore Charles Wager's flagship. It was his expedition that sunk the *San Jose* in battle on June 8, 1708.

The difficult part was installing five hundred meters of cable for the side-scan sonar on a windlass. "We were testing the equipment off the coast of Jupiter, Florida in five hundred feet of water," Weller explained.

The *San Jose* project team now grew to include veteran salvagers Joe Kimble, Doug Gossage, Bill Brom, Brad Williamson, and Bob Weller. The men learned how to use each piece of equipment independently and although assigned different responsibilities, each knew the other's job aboard.

The first trial run with the Edgetech side scan went well until the team tried to reel the towfish back to the surface. They had obtained good images of the bottom.

"It was the end of the day and our Onan generator broke down. We couldn't pull the five hundred meters of cable onto the stern of the boat and we couldn't get the Onan fired up. It was the original generator that came with the Striker and it was twenty-five years old."

Weller decided to give the generator a rest. They could not go into port with five hundred meters of subsea cable dragging behind. Weller gave the generator a last try and it started. They got the cable aboard.

"On the way to the dock Bill Brom said 'Why not buy a new generator?' It would probably cost $10,000 and I was running low on cash. Brom said, 'I'll buy it for you.' Up until that time I never realized Bill was a multi-millionaire. He'd just been a diver. We bought and installed a $10,000 Northern Lights generator."

By the end of summer 1997, Weller's team was ready to tackle the *San Jose* project. "We had trained. Each member of the team knew the other's job. The equipment was working great. All we were waiting for was the lease from the Colombian government."

COLOMBIAN TURMOIL

Weller related the frustration as they were forced to postpone the project as the political situation in Colombia changed. War with guerillas and drug lords waged. Murder and mayhem ruled cities and towns as drug cartels vied for control.

"Margaret and I visited Colombia for a week. They put us on national television talking about how exploration of the shipwrecks would benefit Colombia. We had lunch with the President's brother. He told us that President Pastrana was doing all he could to get shipwreck legislation passed, however, guerillas were active and his hands were tied."

NO LEASE, NO TREASURE. IT'S STILL THERE

Time slipped by. No lease was granted to the salvors and the *San Jose* project never materialized. The armed Spanish galleon remains on the bottom with a fortune in gold and silver.

"I know where it is." Weller smiled as he sank deep into the cushion of his leather armchair, hands folded behind his head. The greatest unrecovered treasure in the world remains underwater. Unrecovered.

10

BACK TO WORK ON THE 1733 FLEET IN THE KEYS

"We started looking for the *San Fernando*," Weller said. The *San Fernando* was a galleon no salvor in the Florida Keys had yet found. It was part of the 1733 treasure fleet.

Weller moved the Striker down to Lower Matecumbe Key where they rented a four-bedroom house belonging to diver Bernie Smith. In February 2000, Weller and his team were using the 37-foot Striker, *Expedition*, prepared for the *San Jose* project, to search for the *San Fernando.*

"We were working off Duck Key and Grassy Key. Lobster pots were the biggest obstacle. We couldn't run a straight line. Our prop would snag in lobster pot lines. Brad Williamson would have to get in the water and untangle them."

"We got a beautiful hit with a lot of potential. The water was so dirty that we didn't even look at the bottom. We put the side-scan sonar over and took a picture of it. It looked good. Because of the bad weather and lobster pots, we broke off the search after two weeks."

The team came back in June 2000. "Everybody wanted to look at the hit we had gotten in February. John Harkins, one of our investors in the project from Alabama, got in the water first. It was nothing but long metal plates with coils of wire on top and hundreds of fish. That ended that potential hit in a hurry," Bob explained.

"We magged an area five by seven miles. Then turned our attention to other wrecks. Don Washington, Jack Haskins, and Joe Kimble had a lease on the *El Rubi Segundo* which was the *Capitana.* I subleased from Don Washington. Bob Benson was aboard as an archaeologist, which was a state requirement. We found a flintlock pistol, cannonballs, fire brick, pottery shards and a few silver pieces of eight."

Amy Wycliff, the daughter of one of Weller's investors, Lloyd Wycliff, had just graduated from the University of California at San Diego. She dove down and found a piece of eight on the edge of a hole. Amy wasn't sure so she showed it to her father who had yet to find a coin. It was a full date 1732 piece of eight.

Dick Holt put a bezel around the coin so Amy could hang it around her neck and they made a certificate with her picture on it that authenticated her find. Amy went home flying on a cloud.

The weather turned bad. The divers were sitting around Bernie Smith's house with nothing to do. "There was a twenty-knot wind. We were out of the water just sitting around with nothing better to do than tell stories."

A TALE FROM THE OLD DAYS

"I told them the story how in 1965 when Ray Manieri and I were working off Marathon. . . ." The story began as most of Bob's tales began. He set the stage dramatically.

"We stayed at Ginger's Siesta Motel opposite the airport in Marathon. That's when I had the sixteen-foot Mohawk boat on a trailer. I went out to hook up the boat. A father and son came out of the motel and approached us." Weller took his time.

"The father said, 'Ginger said you are treasure divers.' Ray answered yep. He then asked 'We're from up north. Where might we look to find something to take back as a souvenir?' We told them to drive north on U.S. 1 to Lower Matecumbe. There was a sign along the road that read 'Yankee Don't Go Home' put up by Eagan Realtors."

"Ray told them if they parked by the sign and walked out into the water they might find something. Ray had searched that area the year before and successfully salvaged treasure from the wreck of the nao *San*

Felipe called El Lerri that sank one mile offshore. He knew there was a scatter pattern that came into shore."

Weller paused then picked up the tale again. "We went diving. Got back to the motel about 6 PM. When we pulled up, the father, his wife and boy came out of the motel with a plastic tray covered by a towel. The father began shaking Ray's hand. 'We can't thank you enough. We parked by the sign and began looking in the water.'"

"He uncovered the plastic tray. They found a dirk, two pillar dollars and two pieces of eight. The father crammed fifty bucks into Ray's hand." Weller was amused by the story retelling it some forty years later.

TREASURE BEACH

"The next day after I told the story of the family's find, Brad Williamson was out on Treasure Beach. It was right at the end of the street where Bernie Smith had his house. I'd gone into Islamorada to rent dockage for the boat and returned about 7 o'clock. Brad came out and met me at my car."

Even the words provoke dreams. Gold and silver that Bob Weller and his dive team recovered from sunken Spanish galleons that wrecked off Florida's coast.

View of Treasure Beach at Mile Marker 74 in the Florida Keys.

Treasure diver Brad Williamson with coins he found on Treasure Beach.

Treasure diver Brad Williamson holding emerald jewelry he found on Treasure Beach.

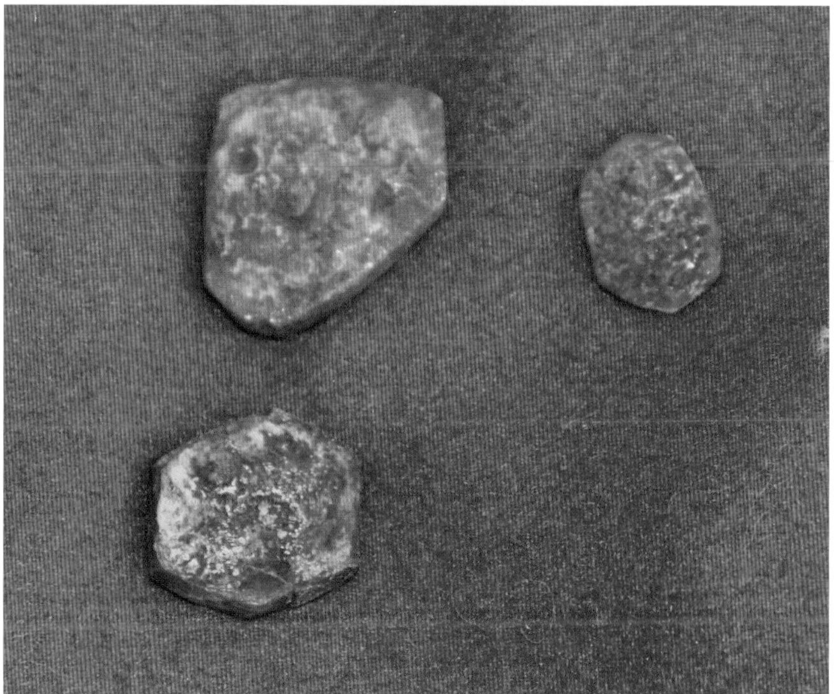

Brad Williamson's coins found on Treasure Beach.

"Brad pulled out a plastic cup. In it was a piece of gold jewelry with four deep green emeralds in it. Brad found the piece about seventy-five feet off the beach."

"I asked Brad if he'd showed it to the others. He said no, so we went upstairs together. I called the other divers around and Brad told them where he worked and what he'd found."

It was dark so the divers had to wait until morning. By morning the weather was still bad and the team was kept in port. They went to Treasure Beach. "Seven of us were spread out with metal detectors wading in three feet of water looking for treasure. We found some musket balls, that's all."

SAN FERNANDO WRECK SITE

The 2001 season found Weller and his team back at Bernie Smith's house. They were working on completing the survey for the *San Fernando*. They explored a few wrecks around Marathon. The divers found a ship that had gone down in the 1800s and uncovered bits of porcelain and glass shards. Magging for the *San Fernando* revealed many other wreck sites.

Weller shifted the operation back to the *Capitana* that had a valid state lease. The divers found two-, six-, and twelve-pound cannonballs. "We found a nice clay pipe, buttons, buckles, pottery shards, a few silver coins and a top from a powder flask. Rob Barfield, one of our investors found a nine-inch diameter intact pewter plate.

"We finished up the survey for the *San Fernando*. We intended to go into the identification phase the next season but a big shark got in the way," Weller said. Another story was in the offing.

"We were in lobster season. We pulled up 95 lobsters in one day. The Marine Patrol came up. As we talked, they told us about a big anchor they found in front of Long Key."

"The Marine Patrol had a handheld GPS and they gave us the numbers. The next day we went looking for it. Aboard were Lloyd Wycliff, Alan Weller, Margaret's son by a prior marriage, Bernie Smith, Stefan Sekora, Margaret, and Lloyd's wife Chris. Margaret and Chris stayed in the boat as we jumped in off Long Key to look for the anchor."

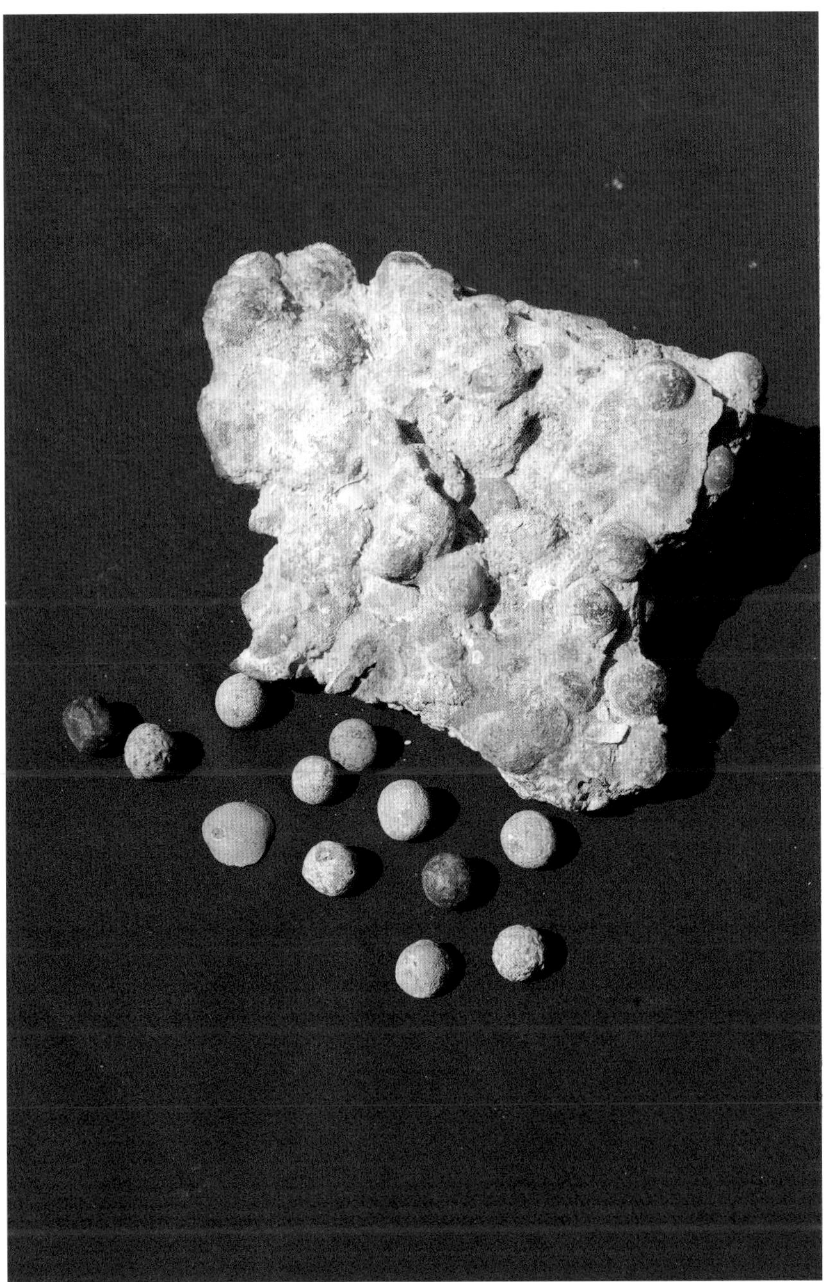

Musket balls found in a clump underwater.

Ocean lifeguard Peter Leo diving down on cannon he discovered in shallow water off Jupiter, Florida's public beach.

"We spread out a good four-hundred yards from the boat but didn't find the anchor. I headed for the 1733 *Almirante* site of the wreck of the *Gallo Indiana*. We had not gone a half-mile when we saw a five-foot stingray jump out of the water. On the third jump a ten-foot hammerhead shark leaped out of the water and grabbed the ray in midair. The shark took the ray to the bottom."

"We pulled alongside and could see the shark on the bottom with the five foot ray shaking it like a potato chip. We watched for five minutes. When Stefan was spear fishing in Marathon a shark had caught him. Luckily

John Christopher Fine detecting on Treasure Beach.

the shark hit between his back and the tank pack. It threw him out of the water. Stefan had a hard time believing the diver's adage that sharks don't bother ya." Weller smiled.

"That was the 2001 season. It was August and the weather turned bad. Most of August we spent going to Treasure Beach. One day Rob Barfield and I were there and Rob found a 6½ inch gold chain and I found two inches of it."

"The next day everybody was on the beach. We pulled up five more sections of gold chain. The longest piece was 28 inches. The total length of all the gold chain pieces was ninety inches. Nice heavy gold chain," Weller said. "That ended the season and we never went back."

11
HOW TO FIND SUNKEN TREASURE

"WHAT I VISUALIZE AS A BROAD SPECTRUM OF THIS whole thing is recognizing that Florida is the epicenter of treasure salvage. Some of the greatest finds in history have been made here on the East Coast of Florida," Bob Weller declared.

When a famous outlaw was asked why he robbed banks, the desperado replied with a laugh, "That's where the money is."

The plain fact is that Florida is where sunken Spanish treasure is. Plenty of it. Despite fabulous finds along miles of Atlantic Ocean coastline, there is still more to be found.

"This has been going on over the last fifty years. More. It started around 1950 and really got going strong the last forty-six years," Bob Weller said.

"The intent here is, there are countless numbers of people that have the American dream: salvaging sunken Spanish treasure." Bob Weller had a point to make and he was leading up to it.

The question was: "How to find sunken treasure?" The thought took Weller on a philosophical diversion. A half century of searching for and finding fabulous sunken treasure off Florida's coast gave him great insight into what it took to answer that question.

"I'd like to focus on the American dream. For the average layman, salvaging sunken treasure is a closed door. They can't get in. They have to realize how tough it is to become a salvager," Bob explained.

Weller Treasure Seminar attendees on board and waiting to put their skills to use underwater. Bob Weller is on the far left (with sunglasses).

"Over the last fourteen years I've been giving seminars on 'Follow Your Dream. Salvaging Sunken Spanish Treasure.' An important aspect of that is I'm the only open door that I know of in the entire U.S. that offers people a chance to go through that door," he said.

"My last active years have been helping people get started. When I pass over the bar I want to be known for that. I want to be remembered for helping people get started," Bob said. His mouth closed and his eyes looked determined.

Bob and his wife Margaret's hospitality to treasure divers is legend. Good food, advice, help, direction, good company, a willingness to share knowledge and great tales of sunken treasure have been the Wellers' hallmarks.

THE MOST IMPORTANT TOOL

"The most important tool is patience. The second is perseverance," Weller said.

Diver Myriam Moran aboard treasure hunting ship with underwater metal detector.

"Nothing beats those. Even without metal detectors we were able to find treasure. When we got metal detectors, we went from nine gold coins the first year to 68 in the second year using detectors."

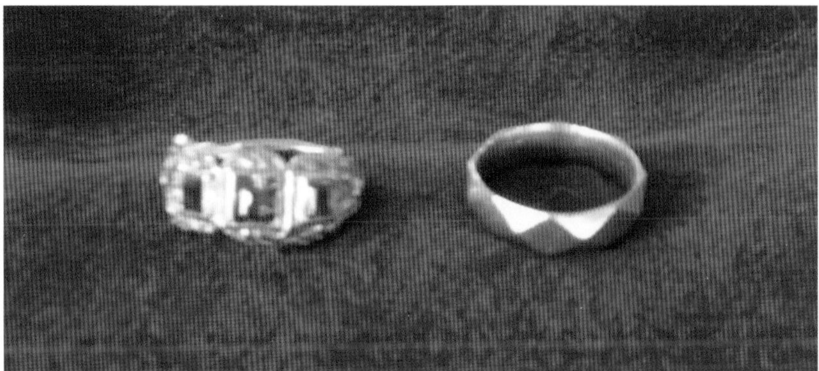

Gold rings found on a Spanish shipwreck site. The gold band became Margaret Weller's wedding ring.

Margaret Weller's wedding ring found on a Spanish shipwreck site.

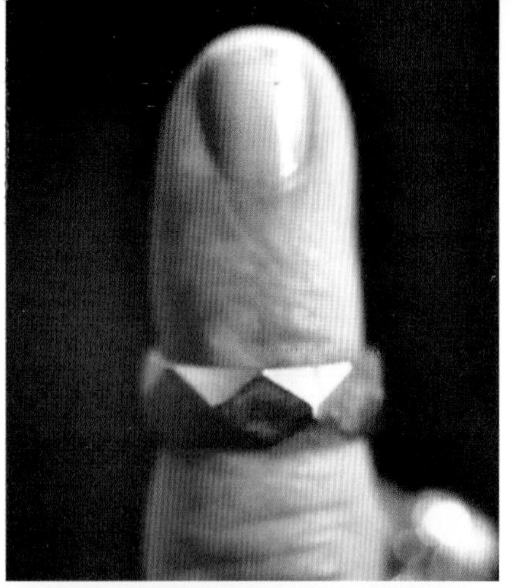

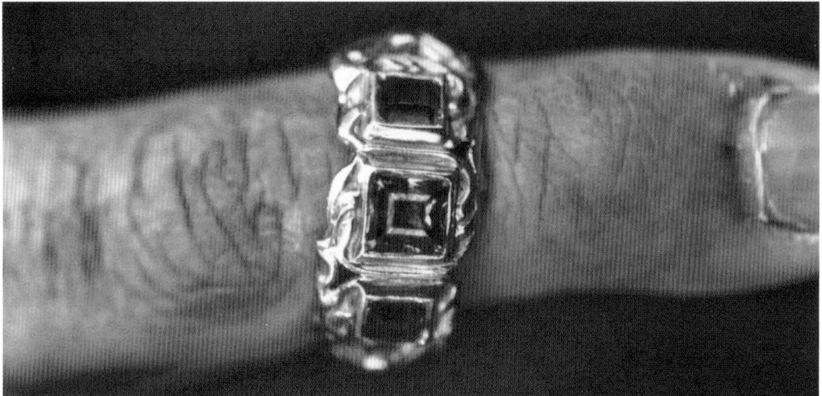

Beautiful example of fine jewelry recovered from a Spanish shipwreck.

"We went from several hundred to several thousand silver coins, from two gold rings to eleven gold rings the year we started using metal detectors. Tools are important but most important is patience and perseverance."

WHAT IT COSTS

There is nothing more discouraging than spending a lot of money to no avail. Everyone has a threshold beyond which an idea, a dream or endeavor cannot be carried through. The lure of sunken treasure has attracted many and there are many treasure hunters. There are relatively few treasure finders.

The ocean is loath to reveal secrets hidden in the depths for three hundred years. What may seem easy at first, once a location is chosen to work, can require a lifetime to find.

Kane Fisher, Mel's son, with his sister, Taffi Fisher Abt.

Mel Fisher worked for seventeen years before he succeeded in finding the legendary Spanish galleons *Atocha* and *Santa Margarita* about forty miles off Key West.

Mel found lots of other treasure, buckets of gold coins, thousands of pieces of eight, so many that his friend and associate Frank Allen handed them out freely from a satchel to publicize their finds.

"I harp on one thing in my seminars," Bob Weller said. "Don't spend money foolishly."

Sage advice but anything that requires a boat to yield access to a dive site, dive equipment, and high-tech treasure finding equipment costs money. Lots of money. So much that Mel Fisher would say, "It takes a lot of silver to find gold."

"I have a lecture in my seminar about how to salvage treasure for less than five thousand bucks," Weller said. He put his two large, work gnarled hands together and lounged back into soft pillows on his patio divan.

Many with the means and the dream jump into treasure salvage without a clue as to what is entailed. Most have no notion of the law and the requirements before even diving into the ocean to look for sunken shipwrecks.

Things have changed since the wide-open days when it was finders' keepers on the ocean bottom; when men like Bob Weller and Craig Hamilton could keep everything they found. Those days are gone forever.

"I direct people interested in salvaging treasure about what equipment to buy. That depends on where they want to go. Most want to produce results early with the least expenditure. They can then build upon that success," Weller said.

The basic stuff of underwater treasure salvage consists of knowledge, diver competency, access to a site or research that leads to a shipwreck. Permission from government, previous lease owners or salvors in possession through admiralty liens is required. Positioning equipment that will enable accurate logs of where searches were conducted, adequate watercraft, dive gear, underwater metal detectors and grit.

All of these will be handled separately. Suffice to say that those with grit, with patience and perseverance, will succeed. Luck follows those who devote themselves to endeavor.

Treasure diving is not a hit or miss, lucky find operation. There have been amazing finds made when people have not sought nor intended to discover a shipwreck. Those are highly publicized but rare events.

An inflatable boat powered by an outboard motor, a simple hookah dive rig with long air hoses, a good underwater metal detector and dive equipment will get a team of treasure hunters started for about $5,000 or less. A complex salvage project requires much more expensive and sophisticated equipment and a sturdy diver support vessel.

LUCKY FINDS, RARE DISCOVERIES

When ocean lifeguard Peter Leo discovered a cannon just off Jupiter Beach, Florida, during his morning swim, it was one of those unanticipated events. Peter Leo donned his swim goggles and headed offshore to swim before assuming his post in the Jupiter Beach lifeguard tower.

He was swimming well on a calm early morning when a school of bait fish drew his attention below. The water was about eight feet deep. Peter saw an object that made him curious.

Sands shift in the ocean. Sometimes objects can remain covered for centuries then a nor'easter, hurricane, or unusual tide can pull the sand away.

Peter Leo with two gold bars encrusted with silver coins. The gold bars were found by John McSherry diving just south of the Jupiter Inlet. Peter is also holding pieces of eight recovered from the same Spanish shipwreck he found in shallow water just off the public beach where he worked as an ocean lifeguard.

Peter dove down. The swim goggles pushed against his face from the water pressure but he got a good look at the long, encrusted tube he'd spotted from the surface.

He swam down again and again until he was absolutely certain of what he'd found. It was an iron cannon. Peter made the discovery of a lifetime. He went back to shore, got a piece of metal, inscribed his name on it, swam back to the cannon and fixed the metal tag to it claiming the find as his.

Peter Leo did the right thing. He was on the telephone all that day to Florida State officials to report his discovery. Nobody responded. There was no one available to come to Jupiter to raise the cannon.

Peter Leo with a crushed copper bucket recovered from the Spanish wreck he found off Jupiter's public beach.

Peter decided to do it himself. He got a barge, enlisted aid and chipped the cannon out of its coral shroud, slung it, and raised it up.

Underneath the encrusted iron cannon was a crushed copper bucket. Peter Leo took that up to the surface then returned to fan the sand by hand. To his amazement he found Spanish silver pieces of eight.

The lifeguard's lucky find resulted in an odyssey. Sunken Spanish treasure found serendipitously, by chance. It was not found by a treasure salvor, rather by an ocean lifeguard on his morning swim.

RESEARCH

There are thousands of shipwrecks on the ocean floor. Modern and antique. Cargo vessels have met their final resting place in storms and sinking through peril and war. It is said that on the Atlantic Coast of Florida alone there are some 4,000 shipwrecks.

Many twisted iron hulls from vessels that never made port. Their cargoes long ago salvaged and the iron hulks stripped of anything of value. Shipwrecks make interesting dives. Their exploration is fun. Shipwrecks are chronicles of time and history.

Sometimes these modern shipwrecks lie on top of or in the vicinity of Spanish wrecks from the colonial period. When that occurs, it makes the salvor's job difficult since sorting out the wreckage can be confusing.

ARCHIVE OF THE INDIES

Primary research about Spanish ships is done in the Archives of the Indies in Seville, Spain. This repository of ancient documents is the source of information about Spain's colonial shipping and trade in the Americas.

Queen Joanna ordered a House of Trade created in Seville in 1503. It was the year of Columbus' fourth voyage to the New World. Functionaries established their headquarters in Seville's cathedral, a righteous place to accumulate gold, quite suitable to the politics of the Church at the time.

By 1519, Charles I created a "cabinet" post at Court to keep track of the discoveries, to regulate trade, appoint governors, captains of vessels, appoint royal contractors and control traffic and events through the King's Council of the Indies.

A building was constructed in Seville in 1572 to house the burgeoning offices and the increased traffic with the New World. Taxes had to be collected, fealty exacted, accounts kept, and shipping regulated. The Spanish required careful records, noted at length in documents carried aboard fleets that sailed to and from the colonies.

The *Casa de Contratación* or House of Trade was overseer of conquest and discovery. They were the clerks and account keepers, the repository for important documents and records, inventories, and salvage reports.

The Archive of the Indies in Seville, Spain, formerly the House of Trade.

The Spanish were good salvors and responded with contractors as soon as news of a sunken ship reached Cuba, their colonial headquarters.

Records and reports of the salvage and the salvors' recoveries, using Indian divers, was all written down and filed with the House of Trade in Seville. The grand stone building is now the Archives of the Indies. It houses the library and original documents preserved from the first conquest of the Americas.

The Seville archives building's portal is guarded by a silent bronze cannon. A magnificent tube presented to Spain's Queen Sophia by Mel Fisher in a gala event that featured a display of treasure the Fisher family and their teams of intrepid divers recovered from sunken galleons.

Not everyone can simply walk into the Archives of the Indies and begin research. The official repository is reserved for documented researchers who can produce letters of recommendation, usually from universities or credible bodies attesting to the validity of their research. Treasure hunters were routinely shunned until many proved to be the archive's most important allies.

Treasure salvors like Mel Fisher, Bob Weller, and Burt Webber discoverer of the *Concepcion*, hired researchers to find records in the archives in Seville for specifics about shipwrecks they were searching for. Bob Marx, the legendary diver that excavated the City of Port Royal, Jamaica, learned to read ancient Spanish script and did much of his own research. Jack Haskins became a leading expert. Haskins' research led many treasure

John Christopher Fine on the Island of San Salvador in the Bahamas at the spot where Christopher Columbus first made landfall on his first voyage of discovery. Thus began the conquest of indigenous peoples of the New World and exploitation of natural resources. "We have a disease," Hernan Cortez is said to have told Montezuma. "It can only be cured with gold." From this island, now part of the Bahamas, exploration and exploitation of the Americas began.

Dr. Lee Spence with some of his archives. Dr. Spence uses firsthand accounts of ship wrecking from letters and reports written by survivors, original maps, and newspaper accounts.

Dr. Lee Spence (green shirt) with John Christopher Fine going over shipwreck locations on navigational chart.

Dr. Lee Spence with glass buttons he found in the cargo of the Confederate blockade runner *Georgiana* that sank off the coast of South Carolina. Dr. Spence discovered the wreck of *Georgiana* and was the first to find the Confederate submarine CSS *Hunley* when he was just twenty-two years old. Spence eventually gave his admiralty claim on *Hunley* to the state of South Carolina.

hunters to wrecks they had been seeking for years. Researchers, like Dr. Lee Spence, spent decades pouring over archive documents to locate sunken galleons.

Researchers found old maps, ships' logs, and testimony from inquests after a sinking occurred. There are witness reports that described where

John Christopher Fine (left) with Bob Marx (black shirt) and David Foster reliving some of Bob's great treasure diving adventures. Bob was a great storyteller and his treasure diving exploits are renowned the world over.

ships went down, as well as salvor's reports that describe where they camped when they used Indian divers to bring up lost treasure.

Invoices for salvage services of Don Francisco Nuñez Melián discovered in the archives by researcher Jack Haskins put researcher Eugene Lyon on the right trail. It was this research that put Mel Fisher onto the area off Key West that led to discovery of his fabled quest. It was the dream of his lifetime, to find two treasure-laden galleons from the 1622 fleet, *Atocha* and *Santa Margarita*.

Documents in the National Archives kept in Guatemala City. Many pages of rare archive documents have been destroyed over 350 years by worms, insects, climate, and water damage.

Archive documents in Seville are written in old Spanish. It is in a script that was in use at the time for official writings. Numbers were written out. The script runs on and on without the benefit of indexes or headings. It is called procesal and can only be read by those trained in deciphering it.

It is not enough to be fluent in Spanish to decipher the ancient scrawls. Many documents have been ruined by worms or water damage; some are missing entirely.

Galleons didn't just disappear. There were records of them leaving Spain, arriving in the Indies, transferring cargoes of goods from Europe, trading for and picking up cargoes of dyes, hides, porcelains from the China trade in the Pacific, gold and silver bullion and coins.

When a convoy of ships left, usually from Cuba where ships arrived after trading with Caribbean ports of Mexico, Cartagena, and Panama, records were made and kept. One copy aboard the ship itself, one on the *Capitana* or convoy master's ship, and a copy left in Cuba in case of disaster.

Survivors and crews stayed with their ships. They camped on beaches, made do with what they could salvage from the broken hulks until help

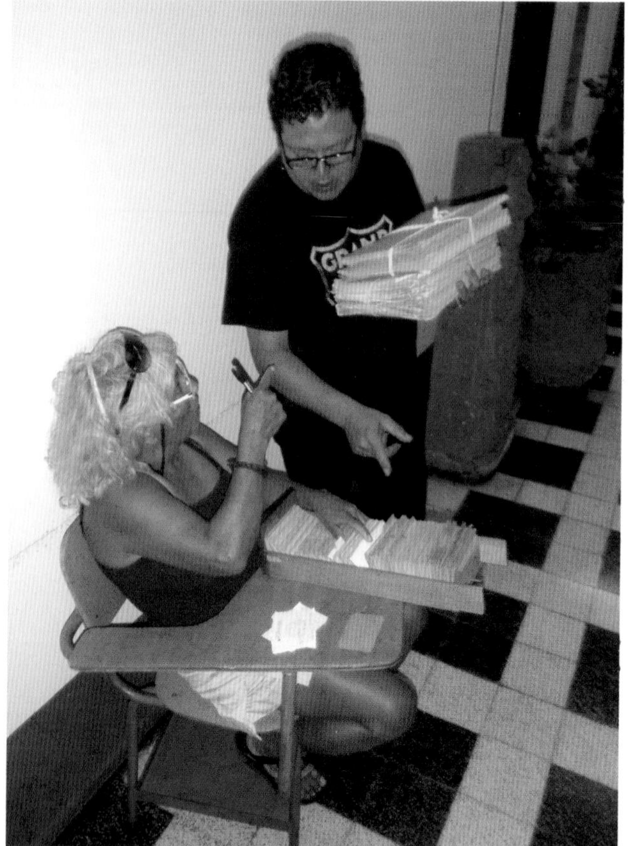

Diver and researcher Myriam Moran with archive documents in the National Archives kept in Guatemala City.

arrived. They would send runners along the beach to the Spanish settlement in St. Augustine, Florida. Courier ships would return to Cuba with the news.

Salvage and relief ships and crews would be dispatched. That which could be gotten out of the sunken galleons was taken, logged in, and returned to Cuba.

There are many ways to short circuit going to Seville and learning to read procesal. However it is done, research is important to identify then locate sunken Spanish ships.

DOING RESEARCH AT HOME

There are three basic fleets that were sunk in hurricanes off the coast of Florida. The 1622 fleet off Key West, the 1715 fleet that was sunk off the coast south of Sebastian Inlet and the 1733 fleet that struck the reefs in the Florida Keys around Marathon. Many other vessels were lost. Some were individual ships that may have been carrying mail or payrolls, passengers, and light cargoes.

Treasure galleons were formed into convoys for safety and protection, armed and escorted by heavily armed warships of the Crown.

The State of Florida maintains a museum in Tallahassee on Florida's panhandle that houses reports from salvage efforts in Florida. This museum and its archives and library are available to the public as are displays of treasure and artifacts that form the state's share of treasure recovered.

Mel Fisher Historical Society maintains a free website, www.fishermuseum.com. The work of Taffi Fisher Abt, marine archaeologist Jim Sinclair, and their colleagues on this website reveal their dedication to making information available to the public. Salvage work conducted by the Fishers, photographic documentation, and research are available free of charge.

Divers can stand on the shoulders of those that have gone before to see what has been done. There are also many important books about Spanish colonial events and treasure salvage. Bob Weller has written books and articles about sunken Spanish treasure. They are excellent reference works.

This is the place to begin. Read, study, learn. "I've written nine books about treasure," Bob Weller said. "It's all there." It is. Information about his exploits and how to find treasure are among the pages of his tomes.

RIGHTS AND PERMISSIONS

Before the passage of federal legislation, called for short the Abandoned Shipwreck Act in 1988, salvors could file a claim in admiralty.

Admiralty jurisdiction in the United States is vested in District Courts generally in the judicial district where the shipwreck was found.

Salvors who discovered remains of a sunken vessel or shipwreck site, before the passage of the Abandoned Shipwreck Act, would recover an object from the bottom, present it to the Court and request the vessel be arrested.

Court documents would vest possession into the hands of a U.S. Marshal. Salvors would then request the Court to appoint a substitute custodian, usually the salvor.

An admiralty claim afforded the salvor protection of the U.S. Courts. If poachers menaced or went diving on the shipwreck site, the salvor could call in the U.S. Marshal's Service and alert the U.S. Coast Guard.

Mel Fisher filed, and his family maintained, admiralty claims to many shipwreck sites along Florida's coast. These claims are "grandfathered" in. They were filed before the passage of the Abandoned Shipwreck Act signed into law on April 28, 1988. The Act, Public Law 100-298, can be found in the U.S. Statutes as 43 U.S. 2101-2106.

Once the Abandoned Shipwreck Act took effect, Congress vested all rights to shipwrecks of historic or archaeological importance in the states.

This means that every state can claim right, title, and possession to vessels within its territorial waters. State territorial waters generally run from the high-water mark of the ocean and extend three miles seaward. Territorial claims are complicated where islands are present that may extend state jurisdictional boundaries.

The Act includes navigable lakes and rivers for inland states and deprives the federal courts of classical admiralty jurisdiction over abandoned shipwrecks that fall within the jurisdiction of the defined vessels.

States have established various protections under the Act and may or may not be predisposed to work with treasure divers or people who make casual finds underwater.

Florida requires a license from the state to search for shipwrecks within its territorial waters. If a shipwreck site is discovered then it must be reported and another license is required to explore and exploit the wreck. No excavation of the site is permitted without express contractual regulation by Florida officials.

What does this include? Every Spanish colonial shipwreck in Florida waters. Those shipwrecks that are being worked under old admiralty claims require written permission from the salvor in possession.

The 1715 shipwrecks south of Sebastian Inlet, for example, have been almost exclusively under the aegis of the Fisher family. Yearly contracts are made with interested and qualified salvors who can demonstrate their responsibility and have the requisite support vessel and equipment. The Fishers adhered strictly to Florida State requirements for reporting and accounting for finds as well as accurate mapping and positioning of areas worked. The Fisher family transferred ownership in 1715 admiralty claims to others, who continue operations with sub-contractors.

As Bob Weller said, there is a narrow window of opportunity for the budding treasure salvor.

LUCKY SALVORS

"I gave that lecture about getting started in treasure salvage during a seminar attended by Joe Peters and Ken Nehiley. They met at my seminar, teamed up and for less than $5,000 got the equipment together and obtained a sub-contract from the Fishers," Bob Weller said.

"They started work on the Cabin Wreck. Found a few cannonballs the first year. The second year they found silver coins. The third year they found gold coins as well as silver coins."

Having the appropriate permissions and contracts in hand in a waterproof container aboard the salvage vessel is imperative. The Fishers patrolled their admiralty claim sites and even used aircraft on occasion. Vessels salvaging for them under contract were required to display contract numbers.

The Fishers worked out a relationship with the State of Florida. The state comes in for the division to take any rare or unusual artifact as part of their 20 percent cut.

Do not try to sneak in without a permit or permission. It is illegal and many divers have been arrested and had their equipment confiscated because of ignorance of the law or by flaunting it.

FEDERAL JURISDICTION

Federal jurisdiction remains from three to twelve miles. A control zone extends even further out to 300 miles. This can mean that depths increase in federal waters to the point where salvage off Florida's coast in impractical save for the most sophisticated treasure hunter with deep ocean capability. Shallower offshore areas in the Florida Keys, beyond the State's three-mile limit, have been accorded environmental protection. These areas cannot be worked without special permissions even though they are in federal waters. Many are within jurisdiction of the National Park Service and part of the Florida Keys National Marine Sanctuary.

FINDING TREASURE AND RETURNING TO WHERE IT WAS FOUND

Navigation is much improved since the days when Spanish galleons sailed within sight of land along Florida's coast until landmarks told them to veer east and cross the Atlantic around Cape Hatteras.

Small handheld GPS units that receive signals from Global Positioning Satellites give accurate readings to within about ten feet and even closer.

GPS readings are in longitude and latitude. The digital numerical read-out enable divers to return to a site day after day, year after year with pinpoint accuracy.

Treasure divers never liked to leave a buoy on their site. It was always an invitation for pirates to jump the claim and work it while they were away. At the same time, it was very difficult to take bearings from land with great accuracy, especially if the site was way offshore.

To obviate the problem of sight bearings, many of the admiralty claimed sites were established by markers on the beach. Pipes, wooden pillars, and colored markers nailed to trees were used. Boats working offshore could take bearings through a sextant on these markers, record the angle of the readings in the vessel's log, and return to the same or almost the same spot again.

The trouble with this procedure was that kids often used the markers as targets for vandalism. Pranksters would move the markers along the beach.

Today, small waterproof GPS units, that cost less than $150, are effective and accurate.

RECORD KEEPING

Records are required to be kept by the State of Florida. Artifacts must be tagged, numbered, and logged. The GPS location where they were recovered must be noted. This procedure is also required by the Fishers and their successors in order to comply with and enhance the reporting system every season.

A vessel log is required for each day's navigation and time on site. The log includes who was on board, the area worked, the conditions, the number of holes dug or blown and their locations and what, if anything, was found.

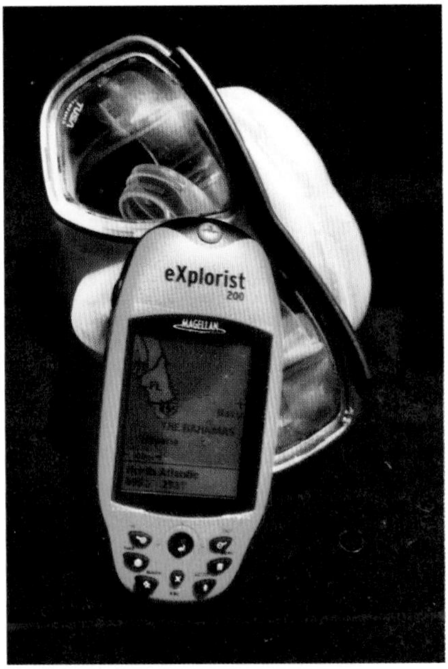

With improvement of computer chip technology many handheld GPS (Global Positioning Systems) devices enable accurate pinpointing of locations on land and sea. Most cell phones contain GPS as well.

Careful record keeping is a must. Failure to accurately record the sites worked means that salvage will proceed in a haphazard fashion and the same locations crisscrossed and others missed.

A person with neat, clear handwriting should be designated as recorder. The record should be made in waterproof pen. Records should be kept in waterproof containers when not being used.

TOOLS OF THE TRADE

VESSELS

There are two aspects to a dive vessel. One is to get the divers to the site, the other is a work boat. Most any watercraft can transport divers to a site given proper ocean conditions. A work boat is used to tow and support

Bob Weller with *Pandion*. This ship was a lucky boat. Many of its voyages resulted in treasure finds.

search equipment and when an area is selected, to not only support divers in the water but to support equipment used to excavate the shipwreck.

Some treasure divers have been successful using a simple rubber inflatable boat with an outboard motor. Some have even devised a prop wash deflector for the outboard. In most cases, however, divers who get on site in an inflatable or small run-about are often limited to simple excavation equipment.

When working a shipwreck in relatively shallow water, an outboard powered inflatable can carry a gasoline powered generator. The generator will run an electric water pump. A simple inexpensive pump will draw ocean water into the intake and send a powerful stream down a hose providing a water jet below.

Innovation is key to underwater exploration. "The boat that you use depends on the depth you are working in. You can't work close to a reef with a mailbox," Bob Weller said.

"The waves bounce the vessel up and down and the mailbox will strike bottom and knock the stern off. That's why in 1994, I used jet boats close to the beach in water two feet deep. We were able to blow sand away with them," he explained.

"For deep water wrecks you need a big boat. Propulsion is needed from the propeller through the blower to reach the bottom. A 25′ boat will probably blow sand at a max depth of 25'. A 50 to 60' boat will blow sand away at depths of 50 to 60'. The blower only vectors the force of the prop wash downwards instead of backwards," Weller explained.

A vessel should be chosen based upon intended use and operational conditions. Vessels working offshore on Florida's shallow reaches usually are equipped with mailboxes or prop wash deflectors.

Dive support vessels are equipped with three large Danforth anchors that can bite into and grip the sand for a firm hold. The anchor line is polypropylene. It floats and has other qualities like not stretching as much as other lines. Boat operators can see the line in the water and know where their anchors are in relation to the vessel.

The bow anchor is dropped forward of the site to be worked and in a direct line with it. The vessel usually has a small inflatable raft or a dinghy that can be used to row out the stern anchors. The vessel is backed down on the bow anchor. When the ship is over the site to be worked, the stern anchors are rowed out on either side and behind the ship. Stern anchors are controlled by winches. With a three-point mooring, the vessel can be moved around simply by cranking in on the anchor lines, backward, forward, and from side to side.

UNDERWATER BREATHING EQUIPMENT

Treasure divers stay underwater for long periods of time. Time is lost if they have to surface to change tanks. They usually use hookah rigs that are supplied compressed air from a gasoline powered unit aboard the vessel.

Hookah rigs usually have long hoses connected to regulators so the diver below can work comfortably thirty- or forty feet from the ship with an unlimited air supply.

Treasure divers use scuba tanks, but the inconvenience and the space they take up on the vessel, the need to get them refilled every day, and the bulk makes them inconvenient compared to hookah rigs. Hookah rigs are limited by the relatively shallow depths in which they can be used. A rule of thumb is 25' depths or less for most hookah rigs.

MOVING SAND UNDERWATER

Spanish shipwrecks have been on the bottom some 350 years. In that time the wooden hulls have disintegrated. Their superstructures were destroyed by hurricane force winds and gales or the effects of ocean waves battering them. Wood that may have remained exposed has been eaten by teredo worms.

Heavier objects will have settled down through the sand into coral bedrock. Sometimes this means that thirty feet of sand must be moved away before the coral substrate is exposed. Moving sand is a difficult undertaking.

THE SCOOTER

Never designed for treasure hunting, the simple diver propulsion vehicle (DPV) equipped with a propeller is sometimes used by treasure hunters to blow away light layers of sand or overburden covering a shipwreck site.

The scooter is simply turned so that the nose is placed against the diver's body and the propeller is aimed at the sand. It is a crude device but it works.

Scooters can be used effectively underwater to move sand.

HAND FANNING

Divers can move small amounts of sand by fanning with their hands. Some divers use a ping pong paddle for this purpose. It is tiring but has the effect of clearing away sand slowly especially when delicate pottery, porcelain, or fragile glass items have been located.

WATER JET

Commercial divers use a fire hose connected to a powerful compressor to dig under shipwrecks or buried pipes or to dislodge objects underwater.

A fire hose puts out a powerful jet of water that can burrow deep into sand or mud. It can destroy fragile objects and may be too powerful for a treasure hunting operation.

Smaller, less powerful water jets can be useful to dig through worm rock or hard sand initially. Care must be taken not to disturb the layer where artifacts are to be found.

MAILBOX AND PROP DEFLECTOR

Two devices have been designed to divert or vector the support vessel's propeller wash downward. Everyone has seen the propulsion from a ship's turning propeller. It is the force that drives the ship forward sending water backward.

The mailbox is nothing more than an elbow that descends on hinges to cover the ship's propeller. Where a boat has twin screws, two mailboxes are often used.

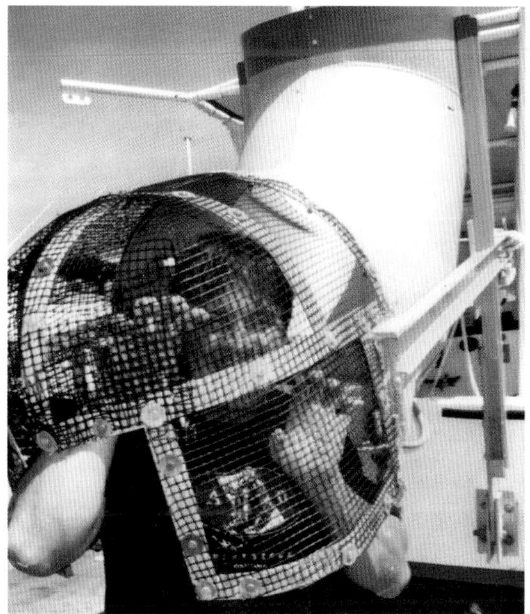

Diver Brad Williamson joking around behind cage of mailbox on *Pandion*. The wire cage covers the ship's propeller to protect divers. The device is lowered down over the ship's propeller, fastened in place, and with the boat securely anchored with as many as four anchors on each point, the propeller is engaged. Its wash sends clear water down to disengage sand in the wreck site work area.

Mailboxes or elbows designed to be lowered over a ship's propeller enable operators to blow sand away from underwater sites. John McSherry on his vessel *Tailhook* with blower.

The vessel is secured using the three-point mooring system described above. The mailbox is bolted into place. A welded cage covers the prop to prevent a mishap if a diver gets sucked against the prop by the force of the water flow.

When the ship's engine is engaged and shifted into forward gear, the vessel does not move. The wash from the propeller shoots down the elbow or mailbox and blows sand away, at the same time digging a round hole in the bottom.

Divers work around the perimeter of the hole with their metal detectors to recover artifacts dislodged by the prop wash.

A prop deflector is a crude sand-blowing device. It is simply a steel shield that is lowered over the propeller that directs the prop wash downward.

THE AIR LIFT

An airlift is simply a large underwater vacuum cleaner. It works on the principle that a jet of compressed air passed into a tube creates a force that sucks water into the lower end of the tube.

Air lifts are simple to construct. They are generally made from 4" to 6" PVC plastic or aluminum pipe that is from about 9' to 12' long. A valve fitting is fixed into the lower end of the tube about a foot from the opening. This is the working end. An air hose is clamped in place and secured to the pipe.

A shipboard air compressor is started, and the air is directed through a nozzle inside the pipe toward the opening.

As the air lift is passed back and forth over a sandy or muddy bottom, the overburden is sucked away up the tube and out away from the work site.

A diver operating an air lift can see coins and other objects as they are exposed and pick them up. If the air lift is not used correctly or is too

Airlift being handed down to divers working the wreck of the HMS *Association* off Land's End in the Scilly Isles.

Airlift in use underwater on the shipwreck of HMS *Association* off Scilly Isles.

powerful, coins and other objects are shot up the pipe and spewed out the open end.

In most cases an air lift is adjusted to suit the underwater conditions. Care must be taken not to allow the diver's hand or dive gear to be sucked into the airlift as this can cause serious injury.

METAL DETECTORS

Metal detectors for land use can be bought in an electronics chain store for about $50. They work. Neither the coil nor the unit can get wet. More sophisticated metal detectors cost more.

To work underwater the metal detector must be housed in a waterproof case. Plastic in various forms is used and the unit becomes self-contained, powered by batteries.

Remember that if the batteries are rechargeable, they must be given time to vent the build-up of hydrogen gas before the charging port is sealed.

Be sure to make a large sign that is affixed to the detector so that you do not forget to replace the battery compartment plug before taking the unit into the water. Hydrogen gas in the presence of any spark is explosive. Always give rechargeable batteries time to air.

Treasure hunters prefer battery powered units that can be changed at sea. Only the most sophisticated treasure hunting ships have 115 v electric power aboard to recharge NiCad batteries and power electronic equipment. This is an important consideration when purchasing a metal detector. Autonomy on site is important. Divers cannot come to the surface, pull anchor, and return to port to recharge batteries. Disposable batteries are also an option. They are more costly in the long run but extras can be stocked aboard ship.

Metal detectors are not simply magnetometers. Mags detect iron and magnetic objects only. Metal detectors are pulse induction detectors. The detector is equipped with a housed computerized unit and a coil.

The coil sends a pulse or signal out many times a second. That pulse can penetrate sand to a certain distance. It may penetrate a foot to ten feet and return a signal depending on the sensitivity of the unit and the size of the electrically conductive object below.

When the signal strikes an object that conducts electricity or is magnetic, it returns a signal that is interpreted by the detector.

Detectors have been modified by treasure salvors to serve their specific needs underwater. Some divers do not like earphones underwater. Earphones can be blown off the diver's head while working under a mailbox. They are also somewhat fragile and uncomfortable to wear underwater.

Care must be taken to unscrew an access plug to permit water to enter the earphones so as not to trap air in them at surface pressure. Earphones are not handy when worn over neoprene hoods and mask straps.

Diver Myriam Moran using metal detector on beach near site where Spanish galleon wrecked offshore.

Some divers therefore prefer a modified audible signal that attaches to the sound connector of the detector and emits a buzzing signal. The small, round sound conducting disk is placed in back of a diver's ear, under the mask strap. It transmits a buzzing noise to the bone behind the ear. The device is pretty durable in the marine environment.

"You want one that has very few bells and whistles. No knobs to adjust, high, low or in between," Weller explained. "No needles to wiggle at you. One knob to turn it on, adjust the sound level and use it the rest of the day."

"Discriminators on metal detectors are worthless underwater. You pick everything up. You don't leave anything on the bottom. I found a nice gold coin under a beer can one time." This is expert advice.

Metal detectors often have discriminators that enable divers to tune the detector to eliminate unwanted metals such as aluminum cans. Underwater there are many objects on a wreck site including modern debris and fishing sinkers that produce signals. The problem arises once a detector is tuned, to discriminate some unwanted objects, it may then fail to detect small gold coins and gold chains.

For underwater work the simplest detector works best. It takes time to get used to how a particular metal detector works. Charles Garrett, one of the pioneers in metal detector manufacturing, suggests that it requires

The Garrett Infinium underwater treasure detector. Ultimate engineering used by divers to locate metal objects underwater. State-of-the-art electronics indicates even small gold and silver objects.

at least fourteen hours to get used to a new detector. Once a diver knows how a detector responds to buried objects on the bottom then that detector becomes a useful and reliable tool.

Underwater metal detectors cost from about $1,000 to $1,800. The costliest part of treasure salvage is getting to the right underwater site. Detector failure or misuse on site means that important and valuable objects will be overlooked.

The Garrett Infinium underwater detector is waterproof to 200 feet. It can be used with disposable or rechargeable batteries. The Garrett Infinium underwater detector can also be used on land and in the surf. The advanced pulse induction technology with salt and ground mineral cancellation makes it ideal for ocean exploration.

Some detectors cannot be used where there is salt content or magnetic sand or minerals. Garrett's engineers have overcome this problem. The Infinium emits 730 pulses per second with advanced technical engineering to make it one of the most reliable and advanced underwater detectors available. Pulse induction technology enables any electrically conductive object to be detected, not just magnetic objects. Information can be obtained by visiting their website at www.garrett.com or calling them for information at 1-800-527-4011.

MAGNETOMETERS

Magnetometers, mags, detect iron objects. As the name implies, they detect ferrous metals. The larger the object, a galleon anchor or a pile of cannon tubes, the easier it will be for a mag to detect them.

"It took Mel Fisher two years magging before he found his first galleon anchor. He covered a lot of ocean," Weller said. He explained how they work:

> *There's a can of pure kerosene. It has ions in it. You pass an electric charge through it and they align themselves plus and minus according to the charge that goes through it. There is a pulse every three seconds. When the mag is pulled through an area of a shipwreck the iron objects create a magnetic field. The particles within the mag shift to that field. Every three seconds the signal straightens those electrons out. This*

Diver Brad Williamson operating search boat, towing a magnetometer. His concentration is on a screen that shows bottom scans.

Hunting for shipwrecks requires long days of searching with side scan sonar and magnetometers. Cable is being played out on a towfish attached to a side scan sonar unit.

creates an electromagnetic force. An amplifier aboard ship monitors the shift and it shows up.

Magnetometers are towed behind treasure search vessels. The search areas are recorded on charts. The vessel must be kept on course so as not to miss areas and not to go back over areas previously magged.

In the area off Key West where Mel Fisher discovered the *Atocha* and *Santa Margarita*, towers were established in shallow areas. Divers with binoculars would take turns manning the towers and use radios to give directions to the search boat to keep it on course.

SIDE SCAN SONAR

Sonar emits an acoustic signal that strikes an object under the sand underwater and bounces back. The signal is interpreted by a shipboard computer. An image is actually drawn of the object underwater.

A towfish is pulled behind the search boat. The towfish emits and receives the acoustic signals. Cables connect to the ship, attached to a sophisticated and very costly computerized base unit.

Because of the cost and relative sophistication of side scan sonar, only well-financed treasure search expeditions use them. Similar to radar, an actual image appears not only on the screen, but it can be generated in a printout.

Side scan sonar units are tied into GPS navigational systems so that the shipboard computer not only records the image, but it gives the exact position where it was received underwater. Divers can return to the spot and search the hit.

CARE OF EQUIPMENT

Dive equipment is expensive. Saltwater takes its toll on gear. Corrosion and dry salt crystals can quickly ruin sensitive equipment. A freshwater rinse bucket or cooler full of fresh water on board the salvage boat is a handy way to store metal detectors and cameras between dives.

It is not enough to give equipment a fast rinse with a hose after diving. Sensitive electronic equipment, underwater cameras and strobes should be soaked for several hours in fresh water and stored inside out of sunlight.

When the gear is not to be used for a period of time then a cap full of white vinegar added to a five-gallon rinse bucket will help remove salt crystals. After the equipment is soaked for several hours in the vinegar water it should be rinsed thoroughly with a hose to remove vinegar residue.

DOCUMENTING THE FINDS

Photography is an important tool to document and identify objects underwater and on the surface. A picture is worth a thousand words, the old saw goes. It is true. Bob Weller and his teams carried cameras aboard all the time.

Taking and sharing photographs is also part of the joy of diving. Finding treasure is an experience of a lifetime. Having a camera ready to capture the moment is important.

Digital cameras are easy to operate. Waterproof housings are available to take them underwater. Some digital cameras are made to be waterproof without a housing to depths of about thirty feet. SeaLife self-contained

The SeaLife Micro 3 digital underwater camera. It incorporates state-of-the-art electronics, high resolution, and the newest digital technology in a palm size, easy to use camera that can store upward of 8,000 photos. Pictures can be deleted as desired to clear memory.

The SeaLife Micro 3 digital camera alongside the Nikonos V film camera. A dive mask gives size proportion.

underwater cameras are simple to operate. The SeaLife rubberized case is rugged enough to withstand shipboard use. It is good to keep a waterproof camera aboard ship to capture precious moments. Film has been largely replaced by digital photography and few people still use underwater film cameras. Many camera models offer still photography as well as video, another way to save the action.

Documenting finds and capturing the thrill of a lifetime at the moment of discovery of sunken treasure is well worth the time it takes to master the essentials of underwater photography.

IDENTIFICATION AND PRESERVATION

"Where did you find that?" Simple enough question but hard to answer in the open ocean. Records must be kept and artifact sheets properly filled in.

The practical reason is obvious. Treasure divers want to return to the same place to search for more. While this seems obvious, many divers get so excited at a find that they pull anchor, take vague readings off a beach, and head into port with their treasure.

Can they return to the same spot underwater? Maybe, maybe not. Maybe the seas and weather will turn violent, and it will require days before they can get out again. Vague memories of where an object was found are clouded when time passes. Many great finds have been lost to the frailty of human memory. Clear and precise record keeping and GPS readings are imperative.

ARCHAEOLOGY

This is not a text on underwater archaeology. Suffice to say that objects recovered must be handled appropriately. Fragile and delicate items, especially earthenware and porcelain, leather, wood, paper, and ivory objects must be immediately immersed in fresh water on board the vessel. Keeping a delicate object wet will prevent it drying out and keep salt from crystallizing. Expanding crystals of salt will crack and thus destroy the object.

Treasure divers use airtight plastic bags to keep objects safe. Tags and artifact sheets are prepared.

A pocket watch found on a shipwreck carefully preserved. Iron parts often rust away leaving only brass behind.

Taffi Fisher Abt and the Fisher museums have conservators at work. Conservators not only preserve finds recovered by subcontractors, who must turn everything in, they have special baths and techniques to prevent an object from deteriorating once brought to the surface.

The way an object is handled initially by the treasure diver makes a difference. The object can easily be destroyed. Wooden ship's members, once dug out of sand or mud underwater and exposed can be quickly broken by wave action. Wood is eaten by tropical boring teredo worms.

It is important to notify conservators immediately when objects are uncovered that require special competence to study in situ and then remove.

LIFT BAGS

Lift bags are used underwater to raise heavy objects from the bottom. In the old days fifty-five-gallon drums were used. The drums were filled with water, sunk, then strapped to the object to be raised. Compressed air was then used to displace the water in the drums and provide lift as water was forced out of them.

Today commercial lift bags, like those made by Carter Lift Bag, Inc. in Enumclaw, Washington, and Subsalve USA Corporation in North Kingstown, Rhode Island, make the job much easier. The object, like a cannon, is slung with webbing or ropes, the lift bag filled with compressed air, and the object raised off the bottom.

Putting too much compressed air in a lift bag will cause the object to shoot to the surface. Compressed air expands as the bag rises and ambient pressure decreases. Divers must use caution when using lift bags. A diver must never to be on top of them and never directly under them. If the lift bag shoots to the surface too quickly it can injure the diver. If the slung object falls, it can cause serious injury. Before beginning inflation, be absolutely sure that no dive hoses or gear is entangled in the rigging.

Lift bags are used to raise heavy objects from the ocean floor.

Lift bag breaks the surface. Beneath is a cannon recovered from one of the ships of Napoleon's fleet sunk off Alexandria, Egpyt.

Egyptian Navy divers bring lift bag back to surface. These heavy-duty commercial lift bags brought up heavy cannons from the wrecks of Napoleon's ships sunk by Lord Nelson's fleet off Alexandria Harbor.

Lift bag being used underwater to raise heavy cannon discovered on one of Napoleon's ships sunk in Aboukir Bay off Alexandria, Egypt.

Lift bags are usually equipped with over-pressure relief valves. An important concept to stress, when using lift bags, is that compressed air expands as an object rises in water and the pressure decreases on the way to the surface. The one-way valve releases excess pressure safely so the bag does not rupture.

Subsalve commercial lift bags have a special plunger dump valve. The valve has a push-button knob at the top as well as a lanyard at the bottom of the bag to enable release of air by the diver. Commercial lift bags by Subsalve have 6,000-pound rated strength resin-treated nylon lift straps sewn to the bottom of the bags adding to their durability.

Some bags have open bottoms and can dump air when they break the surface, some are designed to be more constricted at the bottom lip and

Lift bag bringing up heavy basket of artifacts recovered from Napoleon's fleet off Alexandria.

Lift bag with its cargo of treasures being brought aboard the ship.

Subsalve lift bags enable divers to bring heavy objects to the surface. They are equipped with over-pressure relief valves since compressed air used to inflate them underwater expands as the bags ascend to the surface.

Another photo of cannons being hoisted aboard an Egyptian Navy ship with lift bags attached.

will retain air when the lift bag breaks the surface. The lip is held underwater by the weight of the object.

Lift bags are available from Carter Lift Bag, Inc. and Subsalve USA Corporation in a wide variety of sizes and shapes that provide for most salvage needs. Obtain their catalogs and consult with experts at these companies to discuss specific project needs.

Project engineers and lift bag experts can be reached and catalogs obtained from Carter Lift Bag, Inc. by calling them at 1-800-454-3822, website www.carterbag.com and from Subsalve USA Corporation by calling them toll-free at 1-800-466-6962, website www.subsalve.com.

12

THE SPIRIT OF TREASURE DIVING

"It was the boat. Each diver took pride in finding something and adding it to the pot," Bob explained. It is a difficult concept for some to accept. Despite the fact that individual divers might not receive a significant share of the treasure they

Divers David Foster, Myriam Moran, Will Foster, and Chris Foster with Guatemalan diver Roberto Matheu and his wife and daughter relaxing after diving on a shipwreck site.

found, they never hesitated to put their finds into the pot. What they found that season represented personal honor and gained them respect.

"It's a very small community," Bob Weller would say. Friendship, fellowship and fun aboard *Pandion*, and other vessels in an unusual fleet of salvage boats that turn up every year to work as subcontractors with the Fisher group and their successors, is why most divers yearn for the season to begin. This is evident at the annual Treasure Salvors meeting held in Fort Pierce.

TAFFI FISHER ABT

Taffi Fisher Abt, Mel's daughter who served as director of salvage projects for the 1715 Fleet, chaired meetings. Now that Taffi and the Fishers have sold rights to the salvage claims other directors participate. Florida State archaeologists are present to give guidance to salvors. Veteran salvage divers that oversee the operations instruct on recording and reporting requirements.

"There's a whole new generation of treasure divers," Bob said. He was eighty-one years old when he decided to pass the baton to divers he mentored. He remained willing and able to help them solve problems and give advice as the "Dean of Treasure Diving."

WEDDING BAND

"Our first wedding band came off the *El Infante*," Margaret smiled. "It was a small ring. We made copies of it. It had a solid band with a filigree band over that. We donated the original ring to the West Palm Beach Science Museum and it was promptly stolen." She laughed then put her fist on her hip. Her face looked something like a pixie emphasizing displeasure.

"Then when we were working the *San Roman* on the Cabin site, we found this one." Margaret held up her hand showing the ring finger. "We were together working on the bottom when we found it." She looked down at her wedding band.

"We made copies for Bob and for me in high 22.3 carat gold. We exchanged these rings in 1993, the year of the Queen's Jewels," Margaret smiled.

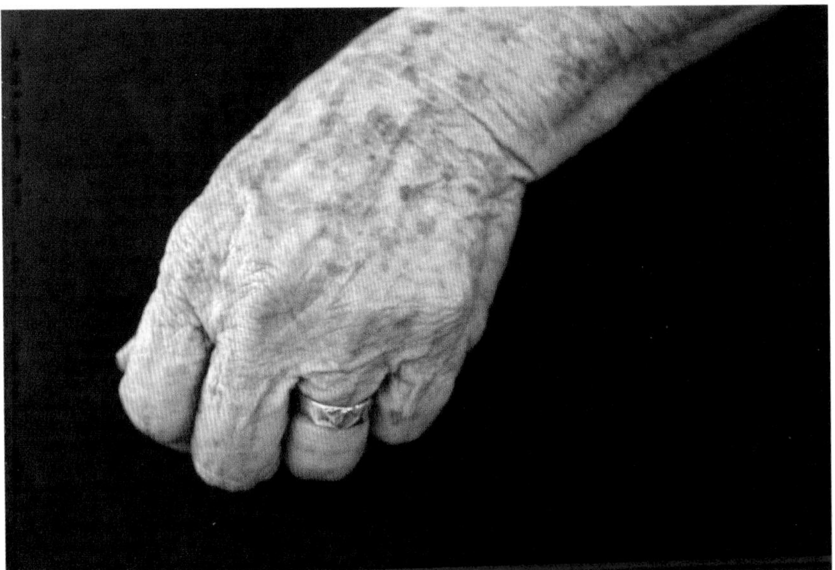

Margaret Weller with the wedding band on her finger. Shipwreck find that became a real treasure as a bond of marriage between Bob and Margaret Weller.

THE END OF THE AMERICAN DREAM

"There's always an end, even to the American Dream," Bob Weller said. He put his hands behind his head, rocked back in his leather swivel chair and smiled his warm, characteristic smile.

Illness forced the Wellers to curtail personal diving activities which did not quell their enthusiasm, teaching, or zeal. Health problems arose that were serious enough to keep both Bob and Margaret out of the water.

Health concerns put an end to their diving but did not end their continuing consultation in treasure hunting projects and participation in exploits with friends.

"During 45 years of bottom time we have filled our bag with good times," Bob declared.

The Wellers' experiences recovering treasure on the sea floor will be "yarned" ashore for many years to come. As long as treasure fever keeps intrepid explorers restless, as new projects tempt divers, the Weller's legacy will remain.

Bob and Margaret received many visitors with many questions. New generations of treasure divers kept them active and participating in research and as consultants.

"When a husband and wife team up to conquer the many problems of sunken treasure, it's a happy union that can only end successfully," Bob remarked. A sentiment shared by Margaret.

HARRY "BIG SPLASH' WISEMAN REMEMBERS

Bob Weller's engineering professor from the University of Delaware recalled the early days diving for treasure in the Florida's Keys. Harry Wiseman was called "Big Splash" in those days by his friend and former student "Frogfoot."

Harry A. B. Wiseman, PhD, described those memorable early years when it was "finders keepers" on the ocean floor and treasure trove belonged to the salvors. His vivid memory tells the tale:

"Bob Weller came to the University of Delaware after service in Korea as a navy seal, full of enthusiasm for scuba and treasure diving. His enthusiasm was contagious. He enrolled in the Engineering School where I was a faculty member. He helped organize a scuba club to train us in safe diving procedures. We had dived in the waters of Delaware Bay. But those waters are cold, even with the wet suits, which we had to make for ourselves. In those days, 50 years ago, we could not buy them from the few diving stores. They were not yet made commercially.

Upon graduation, Bob took a job with Minneapolis Honeywell. But Bob couldn't tolerate living away from diving territory. So, he requested a location change to the Miami area. When a position in the University of Miami School of Engineering opened up, I took the leap. That was the enthusiasm Bob instilled in many people about diving, and it changed our lives. Here was an opportunity to dive in the warm waters of Biscayne Bay and the Florida Keys.

We moved down to Florida and my wife became a scuba weekend widow. On every opportunity we were out diving in Florida's waters. With Bob leading, we explored many old wrecks and recovered eighteenth-century artifacts, such as cannonballs and silver coins. Bob's activities were much more extensive than most of us, and he found many more interesting trophies.

As a side venture, we organized a company to develop an instrument to measure the tremor characteristics of Parkinson's Disease sufferers. With Bob's knowledge of sensors, we designed and built an instrument that measured the arm tremors in patients for the Parkinson's Society of Florida.

Bob also organized free diving spear fishing activities and contests. We brought home our fish, even though they cost us far more than buying from the fishmongers. But it was all fun. And one cannot really fully describe to the lay population the beauty of the coral reefs and the variety of the fish in clear waters off South Florida and the Keys. We did take underwater pictures, but somehow something was lost in the translation. Probably, being right there amongst the animals, burned a more vivid picture into our minds that could not be translated.

Bob organized many diving expeditions, but always with our safety as the foremost rule. So, we survived well. I continued diving until an allergy got me so that I couldn't clear my airways. I had to give up diving, to my regret. But those wonderful memories of our dives with Bob will last forever."

THE NEW GENERATION

Brad Williamson works out. His muscles put oomph into the anchor lines on *Pandion*. His enthusiasm and spirit have never waned since his first encounter with Mel Fisher when he was only a kid. Brad is now in his fifties.

He attended Palmetto High School in Boynton Beach, Florida, the city of his birth. He went to Miami-Dade Community College and the University of Florida for a while. He dropped out. With the encouragement of Bob Weller, he went back to Florida Atlantic University and obtained his B.A. degree in linguistics, majoring in Japanese. He studied Chinese.

Brad took courses at George Washington University in Washington, D.C. studying for an M.B.A. He decided that was not his main area of interest and switched to taking medical courses. Brad worked for Citibank as a conference organizer.

"I knew Art McKee," Brad said. His green eyes showed excitement as he remembered childhood days staying in a house owned by family friends near the McKee treasure museum.

Art was a pioneer treasure hunter in the Florida Keys, the subject of a biography written by Bob Weller. There was plenty for kids to do, playing around Art's treasure museum. At the time, Art was salvaging shipwrecks of the 1733 fleet offshore.

Brad Williamson with his son Hiroki aboard *Pandion*. It is never too early to break in new treasure divers.

Diver Brad Williamson aboard search boat getting ready to head out and "mag" for a shipwreck. Towing a magnetometer behind a search boat enables treasure hunters to find ferrous remains of a shipwreck underwater.

FIRST ENCOUNTER WITH MEL FISHER

Brad met Mel Fisher for the first time when he was twelve years old. It's a funny story and a prelude to his interest in finding shipwrecks.

"Mel Fisher had a kind of pirate ship in Key West. I was a little kid exploring it, having fun as any twelve-year-old would. There was no one there," Brad told the tale.

"There was a sign that read 'Wait for the tour.' No one was around. Finally, I went into the stern and I found a lady. I said, 'Lady when does the tour start?'"

"'You got to pay us,' the woman replied. I had no money. I was leaving the ship when a guy comes up the gangplank. I said 'Mister, I wouldn't go on that boat.' He asked 'Why?' 'They make you pay,' I told him. I was a little brat. The man said 'Come with me.' He introduced me to the lady in the stern. 'This is my friend Brad. He gets a special tour of the museum and he gets one thing out of the museum store. Anything he wants.' The man left." Brad related.

"The woman said, 'Do you know who that was? That's Mel Fisher.'"

Brad chose a treasure map from the gift shop when his tour was over. It got him started. Brad was in the library every chance he got reading books on sunken treasure.

BRAD MEETS THE WELLERS

It was a dozen years later when Brad first met Bob Weller. "I was twenty-three. I had been detecting for treasure on the beaches. There was a metal detecting club in Boynton Beach. I went to the meeting. Bob and Margaret were there."

"That year the Wellers had two operations going. One on the 1715 fleet that was being overseen by Margaret. Bob put an expedition together to work the *Santa Margarita* site under contract with Mel Fisher. That operation eventually fell apart when the person who was to back it financially didn't come through," Brad said.

"At the time Bob was looking for divers since the operation expanded and they had the two sites to work. I said I wanted to dive with him. Bob invited me to a pirate party at his house." Brad remembered the event vividly.

"When I got there Bob showed me around. I was in awe looking at all the treasure and artifacts. Bob asked me if I'd ever seen a silver bar. I said no. Bob tilted back his chair. Underneath it there was a 70-pound silver bar. I tried to lift it nonchalantly. I thought at the time that this guy has so much treasure that he has no place to put it. He's even sticking it under his chairs," Brad laughed.

"We went to work on the *Margarita* project. Bob and a fellow diver, Carl Ward, took a boat down to Key West. They needed someone to take their van down and drive them home. I came after work and started to Key West at 7 PM. I got there at 1 AM. I'm driving in this really bad neighborhood. Bob's directions weren't that clear once I got into Key West. Finally, I heard someone call out to me at a traffic circle. It was Bob."

The divers slept on the boat that night. "I slept on deck with water bugs crawling over my body and the marina lights in my eyes. I was having the time of my life," Brad said with a laugh.

"When the *Margarita* expedition fell apart, I went up to the 1715 fleet. Every day that I was diving with Bob we found treasure. We never got skunked."

It was 1987, the first year Brad started diving with the Wellers. They were working the *Nieves* site, a shipwreck from the 1715 fleet.

"I was down by myself. Visibility was bad, the seas were rough. I was getting thrown all over. Waves and surge picked me up and slammed my mask against a rock. *Pandion* blew a hole. I was working under the blower and got a strong hit with my metal detector. I found my first piece of eight."

"To this day Bob says it's one of the nicest pieces of eight that's come off the 1715 fleet and also a very rare coin. It has 3 date stamps, 1694, from the Lima mint." Brad's recollection was vivid.

Divers got points based on the number of days they worked underwater. Brad did not have enough points that year to get the piece of eight. One of the other divers, Don Kree had the points and took Brad's find in the division.

Brad persisted asking Don Kree to sell him the coin. Don kept telling him no, it was too nice and too rare. "Finally, when Don was buying his house in Boynton Beach he sold it to me," Brad smiled.

Brad's first gold escudo was found working with Bob and Margaret Weller also on the *Nieves* site. It makes a good tale in the telling:

"It was the first day of dive season. The first time we lowered the blowers. The first hole we blew. It was June 1988. Bob and I were on the bottom. I was moving a rock right on the edge of the reef. I cleared one area then went topside to get a metal detector to take a look at the area I'd just cleared," Brad said.

"I got a hit. I found a 1704 gold two-escudo coin. I swam over to Bob and showed it to him. He had a big grin from ear to ear. He gave me a pat on the back and a thumbs up that told me to head up with the coin."

Brad has the two coins still and will never part with them. The story about how he got the gold escudo is one that typifies the Weller spirit.

"Bob never told me he did this but after he turned in the gold escudo he approached Taffi Fisher and said he would like to keep the coin. He would owe her some points but he told Taffi that he wanted his diver to have it. Bob then called each one of his investors in the project and asked them if it would be OK to give me the coin as a gift since it was the first one I found. They all said yes," Brad related the story.

"They didn't find much that year. I took a vacation with Bob and Margaret to New Orleans. We went to dinner. They said they have a surprise for me. Bob took out a black box. I opened it up and there was the gold two escudo that I'd found." The coin is worth about $8,000 today.

"It was very much a mentor relationship," Brad said describing his work with the Wellers.

"This was a very powerful thing in my life that Bob did for me. My first year diving for them I remember sitting on the stern of *Pandion* as she was gently rocking in the waves. I had been diving all day on the *Nieves* looking for sunken treasure. We were heading back in at sunset. I was going to go to Mangrove Mattie's in Fort Pierce on the Inlet. For $2 you got two Coronas and all the hors d'oeuvres you could eat." Brad enjoyed the memory.

"That was dinner. Then I'd go back and stay at Bob and Margaret's town house. It was right on the ocean and I stayed for free. I thought, I want to do this the rest of my life."

He mentioned it to Bob Weller. "Brad this is great but you need to first go back to school and finish your bachelor's degree. Get a career and enjoy this as a hobby," Weller told him at the time.

"I would never have gone back to school if it wasn't for him. People who do treasure hunting full time are living hand to mouth. Bob wanted to see I had an education and a career. He even ordered me to write for my previous transcripts from the schools I dropped out of and have them sent to FAU."

Two divers bought *Pandion* from the Wellers and used it to work the 1715 fleet. They eventually had to sell the boat.

"Bob was the one who pushed me into buying *Pandion.* I was still diving with the Wellers. Bob said it was time I had my own operation. He helped me put the operation together and loaned me half the money to buy the boat," Brad said.

"Bob and Margaret went with me to look at *Pandion.* She was in pretty bad shape. The deck was rotting, she had termites. Age, time and lack of care had taken their toll," Brad said.

"I bought it. Bob and Margaret walked me through the entire operation and showed me how to do it. I stripped her down to bare hull and resurrected her. I resurrected *Pandion*, I didn't fix her. She's out there working again." Only recently has the ship been sold as Brad expanded his treasure operations to deeper water requiring a larger boat.

Brad and other divers Bob and Margaret mentored, befriended, and inspired are the Weller's legacy. The new generation of treasure hunters.

TOP GUN'S TREASURE

John McSherry was a Top Gun U.S. Navy combat fighter pilot in Vietnam. He was born in North Conway, New Hampshire after the United States entered World War II. His ancestors came across from Ireland during the potato famine. They settled first in New Brunswick, Canada before moving to the United States. John's father was an apple orchardist. The lad grew up on their family farm in Maine. "It was ski country in the White Mountains. I competed and won the state ski jumping championship," he said.

McSherry graduated from the Fryeburg Academy, a prep school, then attended Nasson College in Springvale, Maine. He was a junior in college when the war in Vietnam was picking up speed. He joined the U.S. Navy. "After two years of pilot training I got my wings. Started in 1966, got my wings in late 1967 and was assigned to fly F 8 Crusaders. The F 8 was a single seat, carrier based, Mach II fighter. It was specially designed for air to air combat," he explained.

"Most jets were designed to fight and drop bombs. The F 8 was a pure fighter. It was the best. It didn't give up anything. NASA still flies them. They are dangerous. We lost one in three. We had 49 operational losses, only one in combat. The others hit the back of the ship or had mechanical failures."

McSherry wasn't so much lucky as he was a highly skilled and resourceful pilot. "Every plane I flew had a mechanical problem. I became a designated test pilot for the Navy. We had to find out why the F 8 would flame out and not restart in the air. I was assigned with a group of four to find out why. It was a washer on the shaft of the fuel pump that broke off. All started doing it at the same time. Five different aircraft killed guys," he said.

Treasure diver and former U.S. Navy Top Gun fighter pilot John McSherry.

John spoke quietly, remembering his service in Vietnam. He was clearly emotional as he described friends lost. He became a Top Gun because of his reputation as a pilot.

"They knew who was good. Top Gun is an expression in the Navy. If you were good you were Top Gun versus a Plumber which is bad," he laughed.

Treasure diver John McSherry holding U.S. Navy photograph of himself about to get aboard his fighter jet.

Sometimes the Navy would have competitions. The designation was made at the Fighter Weapons School at the Naval Air Station in Miramar, California. John proudly wears his Top Gun cap with mini-golden pilot wings and his Navy lieutenant's bars.

His service career saw his F 8 hit by ground to air fire. McSherry had over 300 carrier landings, 90 at night. "You never get used to them. You come in at 300 knots, just a little over stall. It was the best aircraft ever designed over 300 knots. Under 300 you've given up all kinds of aerodynamics, it is unstable."

McSherry was also designated to attend the Naval Justice School in Newport, Rhode Island. He became a legal officer, prosecutor, and judge. "I was a convening officer. That's like the grand jury in civilian law. At 23 years of age, I was given great responsibilities."

After seven years as a Navy fighter pilot and flight instructor, McSherry left the Navy. He was married and accepted back in college. The drive home found him in the throes of an emotional crisis. They had to stay in a motel for three days. "I couldn't sleep. All I saw was pictures of my dead friends. I left school and moved in with my parents and spent six months in a bathrobe."

Grieving has no place in the life of a combat pilot. "I never grieved. We lost a plane a week and a guy every two weeks. You couldn't grieve.

The job was so high tech you couldn't cry or mope. To stay alive, you had to treat death that way."

He was in several business ventures in Maine until he took over the family orchard in 1979. "You'd have winters off in Maine. You don't grow apples in winter. So, I came to Key West. The idea of treasure hunting got me interested. I talked to a guy at a bar in Key West. He gave me ranges. We found one good shipwreck out there. He'd chart them and I'd go out and find them."

McSherry picked up a copy of Marty Meylach's book, *Diving to the Flash of Gold.* It gave a compass heading to sunken treasure. "We filed an admiralty claim. There's a 1733 bottom that is impenetrable. Nothing from those wrecks goes through it. We were throwing coins into the boat. Thousands of them."

His exuberance was clear. A violent hurricane in September 1733 sent a fleet of Spanish treasure galleons crashing onto the reefs, shoals, and shallows in the Florida Keys. The fury of the storm ripped many of the treasure ships apart spilling their cargoes over miles of the Atlantic Ocean. McSherry contacted the famed archivist and researcher Jack

Treasure diver John McSherry cutting his birthday cake at former home of renown shipwreck hunter Don Washington in the Keys. Don's tiki hut was the place divers came to socialize and split the finds. Don's house became known as "The Bank" among treasure divers. It is now owned by diver David Foster and remains a place for divers to socialize and tell tales of sunken treasure.

Mick O'Connor (sunglasses) with veteran archive researcher Jack Haskins with gold rosary from Spanish shipwreck.

Haskins. "I told him where I was working, beyond the state's three-mile limit. Jack said I have 900 silver bars in front of me."

The year was 1986. Underwater search technology was available but only at a high price. "I called Roy Richie, a pulse induction guy. I told him I needed his help. I wanted him to build me something that could detect a 30-pound silver bar, three to four feet beneath the sand. Roy said, 'It probably can be done. Give me $150,000.' I called Roy from the boat and told him I found a 38-pound silver bar. That meant there were only 899 to go. He was down in two weeks. His car was loaded with electronics. It took me a year to make it operational. It worked. We were working on

Don Washington's admiralty claim on Coffin's Patch. It was the only galleon of the 1733 fleet that had not been found."

McSherry began a meticulous search of the area from seaward to the three-mile limit that was controlled by the State of Florida. State bureaucrats refused to work with anyone in the private sector, sacrificing many important recoveries to destruction from the elements and time. Word got out about his successes working the 1733 fleet. Ocean explorer Herbo Humphries called him. They set up a meeting. The firm had purchased an interest in a Spanish shipwreck located in shallow water just off Jupiter, Florida's public bathing beach.

That's the shipwreck discovered by ocean lifeguard Peter Leo. It was yielding coins and artifacts. McSherry brought his 34-foot Crusader with his pulse induction detector from the Keys up to Jupiter. "The airplane I flew was a Crusader. My boat is a Crusader and it's got a tailhook," McSherry mused from the porch of his canal front home in Key Largo. He named his treasure hunting boat *Tailhook*.

Peter Leo holding two gold bars with silver coins encrusted on them that were found on the Jupiter wreck by diver John McSherry.

He began work with Herbo Humphries' Marex group around 1991. "The first time we took Marex out on my Crusader we got a hit using the PI (Pulse Induction) sled. I put the blower down. I got a hit in the hole with a handheld detector but couldn't find it." *Tailhook* was moved a couple of feet. McSherry located a ship's fitting from the Spanish shipwreck.

Marex wanted McSherry to join them searching for the treasure galleon *Nuestra Senora de las Maravillas* in the Bahamas. After the men worked out a contract, the large Marex treasure hunting and recovery vessel, *Beacon*, left for the Bahamas to set up. McSherry remained in Jupiter working the shipwreck with *Tailhook*.

"One Sunday it was flat calm. The archaeologist they hired was not there. I called Peter Leo. The ocean was like glass. Peter got permission for me to work the site. I found two gold bars," McSherry related. "The Jupiter bars were my first gold."

The four-pound bars had silver pieces of eight encrusted on them. The find was sensational and made headlines all over the world. The lifeguard's treasure was a dream come true.

McSherry left the Jupiter site to join Marex in the Bahamas. "I drove the Crusader back and forth between the anchor and the ballast pile measuring depth. It was a little over a mile long. I discovered a shallow place. My girlfriend Betsi, who had become a crew member, went in over the spot with the hookah rig. I watched her bubbles. She didn't move. The boat was being held by her hookah hose. I snorkeled over to her, dove down. Betsi was holding onto the bottom. There was a fish trap with two nails in it. She moved the trap and there were two pieces of eight under it. I went back to get a buoy. It was way cool. I got back in the water and did a line. There were 10,000 coins there."

Marex sent *Beacon* back to Freeport leaving *Tailhook* on site. They were working twenty-five miles offshore in a single engine vessel. Marex sent a Hatteras out to baby sit while *Tailhook* continued to turn up treasure.

"We were out there alone. We got a hit. A silver bar that weighed two pounds and a few coins, some straight spikes. The unused spikes meant they were aboard for repairs. We determined what we found was a piece that had come out while the ship was bouncing along the bottom. It was a rhythm. I'd be driving the boat counting off and sure enough I'd get a hit and drop a buoy. When Herbo came back with the *Beacon* I showed him the string of buoys and told him each one is sitting on treasure. I told him to go have fun. We found 21 gold bars. A hundred pounds of gold all together. I was satisfied that we'd found the main section of the stern. Coming out of it we found hits in a line."

McSherry decided to follow his instinct. He locked onto due south. "I was eight miles from the *Maravillas*, due south. We hadn't gotten a hit in hours. Then I got a big hit. I thought it was from cables off a boat that hit the reef. A wire rigged clipper shipwreck that was out there. It had winches spread out in the sand."

McSherry continued his search and made several passes over the site where he got the hit. He stopped and told his crew member Betsi to go over side to investigate. She came to the surface and told John to come in. She'd discovered a breach loading swivel gun sticking out of the sand with bronze showing.

"We put the blower down. We let it dig a hole in the sand and got lunch. After their lunch, McSherry dropped overboard. "I thought I was drunk. There was a bronze gun, three elephant tusks, intact Spanish earthenware jars, a silver bar, and some coins. I could make out the writing on the cannon. It read: John and Robert Owyns built this piece Annum 1543 for Enrique Octavus."

"It was a nice hole. There were also three big iron cannons in it. If the ship's bell had been in the hole I would have retired right then and there," McSherry laughed recollecting the great find.

"I told *Beacon*. They came over. I told them that I wanted three days before the *Beacon* worked it. I was going to use the sled with my pulse induction detector and I didn't want *Beacon*'s metal all around me. The spillage line was too long for a galleon. A ship had to hit and this was a first impact on the bottom. I magged the spill line. That's when I found the Tumbaga bars."

Tumbaga is a term for mixed metal. The Spanish adopted it from an Aztec word. The first silver was not pure. Cortez and his men melted it, cast it in sand, and stamped it. It was Cortez' first shipment back to Spain to buy favor with the Crown. Silver melted with other metals without being refined before Spain organized refineries, sent equipment, and established mints in the New World.

"I got three little hits. The sand was easy to move. I found metal bars. They confused me since they were all the colors, black, orange, green. They were impure and contained copper, gold and silver all mixed. My sand wall collapsed. I took 20 bars out of the sand and put them on the boat. One bar weighed 40 pounds. It was very white with oxide and underneath grayish in color."

McSherry wanted to share his excitement with the *Beacon*. He called them on the radio. "No one answered. They were all sick. A bug had been going around. I pulled anchor and went over. I woke up Herbo Humphries and told him I wanted to show him something quick. I took Herbo back to the site," McSherry related.

"Herbo took a metal detector below. He couldn't tune it. Of course, he couldn't tune it. He was sitting on 233 silver bars. The water was only 25 feet deep. We had fun. We kept blowing with the prop wash deflector. We put 50 bars on *Tailhook*. They weighed about 2 tons."

No one really knew the significance of the Tumbaga bars. When they were sold at Christie's auction house, they brought from $700 to $1,000 each. Numismatic expert Frank Sedwick bought most of them.

Disappointed at the result of the auction, McSherry flew to Memphis, headquarters of Marex, and asked for his share of the Tumbaga bars by weight, not value. He received twelve silver bars plus a gold bar that he

Convex side of Tumbaga bar of mixed bullion found by diver John McSherry.

Close-up of a Tumbaga bar of mixed metals including silver and gold.

carried through security at the Memphis airport. "Security loved it. They ran my canvas bag through and all the security people came to hear the story and inspect it."

McSherry found what probably amounts to one of the most important discoveries of all time. He found an unknown ship's impact point and followed the line to the Tumbaga bars. It revealed a mystery since the Tumbaga bars were made in Mexico from 1528 to 1530. One bar was discovered under a 1543 gun. "They may have been salvaged from another shipwreck. Vasquez was Cortez' assayer from 1528 to 1530. He has his mark on the Tumbaga bars."

McSherry hopes to solve the mystery of the Tumbaga bars and one day identify the shipwreck from which they came. He has perfected his detector for another expedition.

"*Tailhook* has had more treasure aboard her than any of Mel Fisher's boats." He stepped aboard his Crusader tied up in the canal behind his house. When he gets his new project together you can be sure that John McSherry will discover more great treasures.

"I'll find them. I like tracking," he said with a smile, determined to finish what he started and bring up the rest of Top Gun's treasure.

JACK HASKINS AND MICK O'CONNOR

Mick O'Connor flew big cargo jets for Federal Express. He's also an experienced Scuba diver with a yen for discovery. His home in the Florida Keys has docking for his dive boat, a perfect platform to run out into the ocean and explore some of Florida's most beautiful reefs. He knows reefs and shoals where shipwrecks have been thrown upon them during hurricanes.

For over three centuries Spain dominated the Americas. After the conquest of Mexico in 1519 and the discovery of riches, the Atlantic Ocean route back to Spain became a golden highway. Fleets of armed galleons and escort ships would gather in Cuba, load supplies, and head north before hurricane season.

Delays in Havana put whole convoys in peril. The 1733 fleet was dashed upon the reefs from present day Marathon northward past Key Largo. The entire previous year's output of the silver mines from South America and Mexico as well as gold in bullion, coins minted in the New World, passenger's jewelry and personal effects, ships accouterments and armaments were lost.

While the Spanish sent salvage boats out of Havana to reclaim what they could, the fury of the hurricane spread wreckage over many miles of ocean. In the early days of salvage, divers began to explore the sunken ships lost to time. Legends like Art McKee, Mel Fisher, and Bob Weller brought up coins and silver bars from the wreckage. Legislation and development of the Florida Keys National Marine Sanctuary put many shipwrecks under government control. Some shipwrecks were claimed

Jack Haskins (brown shirt) with Mick O'Connor with map discussing treasure sites off the Florida Keys. No other archive researcher has accomplished more guiding treasure hunters based on his meticulous research in the Spanish archives in Seville than the late Jack Haskins.

under admiralty law and some of those original claims are being worked today under the provisions of Federal court jurisdiction in cooperation with state and marine sanctuary officials.

Diving is permitted on any underwater site, however, to be able to remove artifacts or treasure, permits must be obtained. Salvage divers continue to work permitted sites following guidelines established for proper archaeology, study, documentation, removal, and conservation of finds. Environmental impact must be limited since some shipwrecks are located in a fragile and protected marine environment.

It is within the framework of restricted and permitted access that Mick O'Connor works with permittees to help bring sunken history back to life. "I guess I was like a horsefly. I met David Foster who had been working on permitted shipwreck sites and had been diving all over the world with well-known ocean explorer Bob Marx. David sent me to Don Washington who had a lease here in the Keys. They told me that a treasure hunter is really a mechanic. The more tools in your toolbox, the more you can do. A magnetometer could see farther that I could see," O'Connor related.

"The first time I went underwater with a magnetometer was on John and Judy Hallas' boat. It was an antique magnetometer judged by today's equipment. Mags are used to find ferrous metals underwater. The first thing they told me was to get my dive knife off my leg. The mag was made to pinpoint iron objects and was unbelievably sensitive."

From that point on O'Connor was hooked. He found divers that had contracts with the State of Florida and permits with NOAA, the Federal agency that has overall governance over the marine sanctuary in the Keys. "I'm from Miami originally. I moved to the Keys in 1980. We worked the *El Rubi, Capitana* of the fleet, with Joe Kimball under Don Washington's permit in 1992. Before that, when I first met Don Washington, I went to his house. He started bringing out coins. He had a ball peen hammer in one hand as if to say, 'Don't touch 'em.' He asked me if I had treasure hunting experience."

Mick O'Connor realized immediately that he couldn't fake it with Don Washington. He admitted he was a recreational Scuba diver with no experience. "Don Washington said he had all the divers he needed. I left him my phone number anyway." Three weeks later, O'Connor received a call from Washington. He asked if he wanted to go to work. Because of his piloting job, O'Connor has a lot of days off together. Washington told him he'd have to be trained on Nitrox. Nitrox increases the amount of oxygen in the breathing mixture. The mixture is adjusted as a function of the depth divers will be working. The usual mixture is 36 percent oxygen as opposed to 21 percent oxygen in compressed air. Twenty-one percent is the same percentage in normal air we breathe, it is just compressed into a Scuba tank.

O'Connor called David Foster back. The horsefly returned to his original host and was hooked up with a dive instructor. He told the instructor that he needed Nitrox training since he would be required to dive three dives a day to eighty feet. There was no time for him to take the course. He was told to read a book and given the precept that on Nitrox the eighty-foot dive would be like a sixty-foot dive.

"I dove all summer with the team on the Juno wreck. We'd fly an underwater sled from the wreck site to three miles off the beach where state waters began." The Juno wreckage is an unidentified Spanish vessel that contained ceramic wares and ship's fittings. A lot deeper than the usual depth of shipwrecks in the Keys, it is located offshore of the town of Juno, Florida.

O'Connor returned to the instructor to get his Nitrox certification. The instructor wise-cracked: "You were diving all summer and didn't die." He made a perfect score on the Nitrox test. O'Connor was ready to work with his buddies on permitted sites in the Keys and began diving seven-hour days underwater. Then he met a living legend in diving and archival research.

The late Jack Haskins with his wonderful, always welcoming smile. Jack was the dean of researchers in the Spanish archives in Seville. His research led to major discoveries of galleons wrecked off Florida's coast and elsewhere in the Caribbean.

Goin "Jack" Haskins was also a pilot. He flew for wealthy people that had their own planes. They had flying in common. Haskins taught himself to read old Spanish. He would spend months in the Archives of the Indies in Seville, Spain pouring through pages of documents. It was Haskins' research that helped Eugene Lyon put Mel Fisher onto the right site that enabled him to find the *Atocha* and *Santa Margarita* forty miles south of Key West. Haskins' research enabled the eventual discovery of the *Concepcion* north of the Dominican Republic in the Silver Shoals. Haskins' research also led to discovery of the *Maravillas* in the Bahamas, according to O'Connor.

Haskins went from research to finding shipwrecks. He had been at it a long time when O'Connor met him. The two men hit it off and remained good friends, although in his later years Haskins no longer went diving. He died at age eighty-three, leaving behind a vast legacy of shipwreck research and important underwater discoveries.

There are many scoundrels in the treasure hunting business. O'Connor once remarked to Haskins that he thought 85 percent of the people involved were dishonest. "You are being far too generous," Haskins quipped. "It's more like 95%."

"They are selling something," O'Connor added. "I don't hang with liars. They want you to invest in something or want you to think they know something they don't know."

That there were seedy characters in the treasure hunting business didn't deter O'Connor. He found good people to work with that consistently labored on permitted sites working closely with the State of Florida and sanctuary officials.

On one of his early dives, many years ago, O'Connor discovered what every diver dreams of finding. The story begins with advice he received from David Foster. "I'd been going out and diving 4 to 7½ hours every day all by myself and finding nothing. I called David and asked his advice. He told me to stop ranging back and forth and do it another way. I skipped the lanes I was going back and forth over the next day and tried to look at the site the way David suggested. I got a hit on a broken piece of a cannonball. I fanned the cannonball with my hand and four inches away I found this golden rosary."

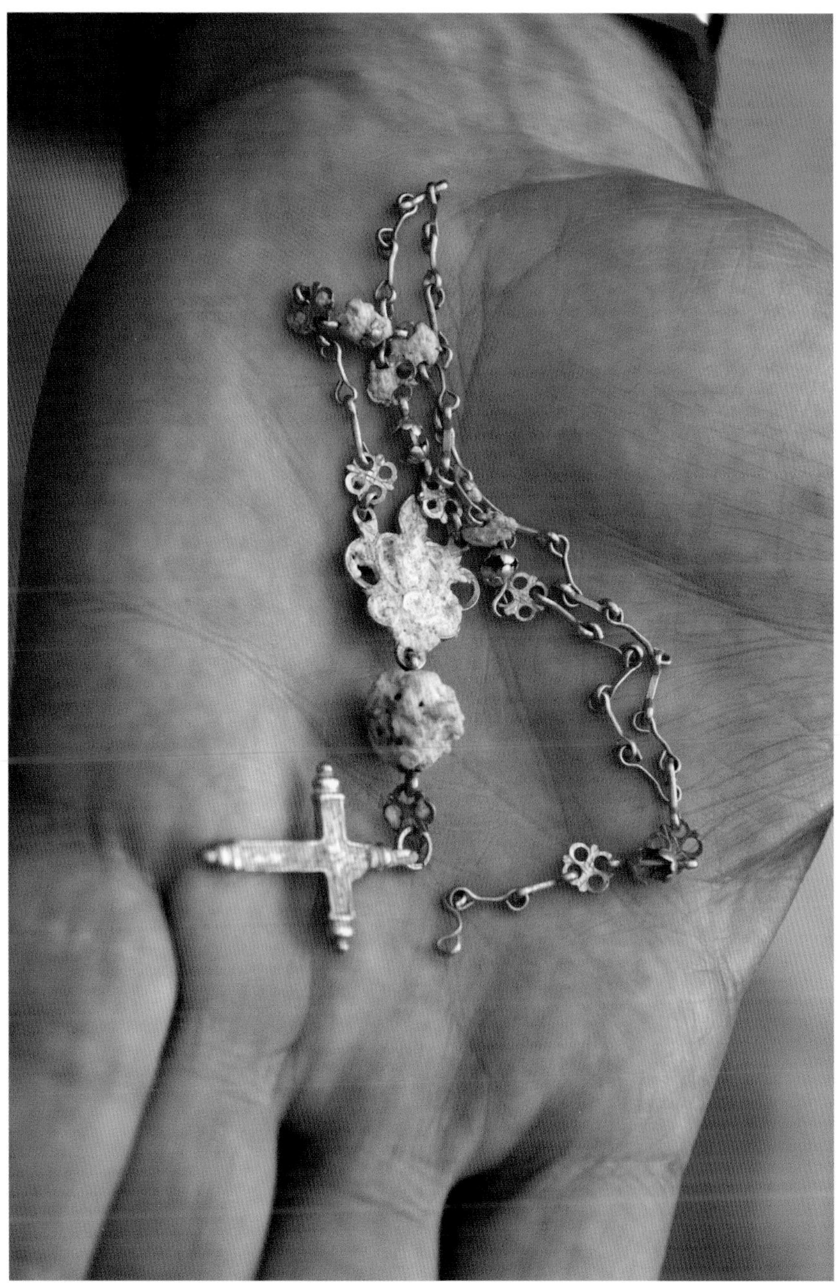

Close-up of gold cross and rosary discovered by Mick O'Connor on Spanish shipwreck in the Florida Keys.

Excitement and emotion were recalled when O'Connor handed the delicate gold rosary to his friend Jack Haskins shortly before his death. The gold was still encrusted with bits of coral growth. Haskins took it in his hand and smiled knowingly, recalling his days underwater.

"If I'd discriminated against iron, I would not have found it. It was just a lucky deal. That was 20 years ago and I haven't found anything significant since then," O'Connor smiled. The rosary was discovered on the permitted *Capitana* site, part of the 1733 fleet wreckage, under Don Washington's permit.

Modern underwater metal detectors such as the popular Garrett Infinium can be set so that poor conductors of electricity are eliminated. Aluminum pull tabs from cans discarded in the ocean, for example, can be dialed out so they do not register. Most treasure divers do not use discrimination underwater for fear of missing small gold objects or chains. Luckily O'Connor kept his discrimination selection at zero. He found a piece of an iron cannonball and next to it was the delicate gold rosary.

Jack Haskins found four Escudo gold coins on the same shipwreck site. Each one was worth $34,000 because of their scarcity. "Jack found one of the richest shipwrecks of all time off the coast of Panama. He did research in the archives in Spain and located the *San Josef*. He had a permit in Panama. Art McKee spent his life looking for the *San Josef*. When Art McKee was looking for the Genovese wreck, Jack told him, 'I'll take you right to it.'" Another treasure tale was in the making as O'Connor and Haskins talked together about their treasure hunting experiences.

"I told Gene Lyon, Mel Fisher's researcher, that they weren't looking at the right site. It's here," Haskins remembered.

Another legend, Chuck Mitchell, one of the original treasure divers in the Keys, once asked Jack Haskins why he never worked the *Atocha*. Haskins' answer was "Who knows." The *Atocha* and *Santa Margarita* were sunk in 1622 with a fortune in gold and silver aboard. The shipwrecks were recovered by fabled treasure hunter Mel Fisher.

The *San Josef*, lost off Panama's Pacific coast, reportedly has $100 million in treasure aboard. Haskins discovered the *San Josef*'s location in 1980. Haskins still wears a ball cap from Panama. He got into diving when he was a pilot for a businessman that was also a diver. Haskins was flying his boss into Bimini. The man had him fly around the island looking for shipwrecks.

Bimini Island in the Bahamas is certainly the place to meet characters. Haskins' boss backed him to go to Seville and do research in the Archives of the Indies. Haskins taught himself to read the ancient Spanish script used in the voluminous records. He found entries giving the location of sunken galleons lost in storms.

"Jack had a black book. We'd go out with him. He'd stand away from us, consult his black book. Then he'd say, 'Go this way.' Then, 'Drop a buoy.' He had the locations of all the treasure galleons of the 1733 fleet," O'Connor reminisced. Legends from the deep.

THE KILBRIDE CLAN

Bert Kilbride was just short of his 94th birthday when he died in 2008. His cremated remains were installed on Neptune Reef off Florida's coast. The memorial bears the legend: "Bert Kilbride, 1914–2008. Last Pirate of the Caribbean." Bert adopted that moniker although he was a benevolent and likable pirate who lived life to the fullest.

Bert had a contract with the government of the British Virgin Islands to search for the fabled wreck of the *San Ignacio*. The ship was owned by the Caracas Company and licensed by Spain to trade in the Indies. The *San Ignacio* sank in waters of the British Virgin Islands in 1742 with a cargo of gold and what is estimated, in today's values, to be $600 million in treasure aboard.

Bert never recovered treasure from the *San Ignacio* although we discussed many plans to return to the waters around Anegada where he was sure he knew its location. Bert ran Kilbride's Underwater Tours on the islands. He owned Saba Rock, an almost barren island where he lived with his fifth and last wife Gayla. Life on Saba Rock was Spartan, the stuff romantic dreams are made of. Bert and Gayla were legends in the British Virgins.

Bert's favorite shipwreck was the Royal Mail Steamer *Rhone*. The *Rhone* was one of the most modern ships of her day. The vessel was at anchor with her sister ship, the *Conway*, in 1867, when the barometer fell. A storm was imminent. The sky darkened and violent winds began to

John Christopher Fine holding 9.4 pound nearly pure gold disk. The disk is not hallmarked with assayers stamp nor was it declared to Spanish taxing authorities. To avoid paying the Spanish Crown's tax on bullion of 20 percent, smugglers carried contraband among returning galleons' cargo. The late Bert Kilbride and the author enjoyed diving together in the British Virgin Islands where Bert owned Saba Rock and searched for shipwrecks on the Island of Anegada.

batter the ships. *Conway*'s captain transferred her passengers to the larger *Rhone*, weighed anchor, and headed out to sea to ride out the storm.

The *Rhone*'s captain also weighed anchor, hoping to outrun the storm. The *Rhone* was steaming around Salt Island hoping to make Road Town Harbor when a furious wind dashed the iron-hulled steamer on the rocks. The ship broke in two. Most passengers and crew of the 331-foot-long vessel perished, and the cargo was lost.

Bert Kilbride explored the remains of the *Rhone* and took diving guests on holiday in the British Virgins diving on the shipwreck. When he first explored the wreckage, some of it was intact. He found the ship's china and serving sets. Bert recovered portholes, fittings, a large copper commercial kitchen tea pot, hand-blown bottles of all sorts, and artifacts that he willingly shared with visitors and diving guests.

John Christopher Fine with Bert Kilbride examining a chart to dive on shipwrecks on the Island of Anegada.

On one dive Bert penetrated the wreckage. He reached down into silt and came up with a tattered shirt. Bert opened the decaying cloth underwater and felt something in the pocket. It was a snuff box with the name Steve Kenyon engraved on it. Kenyon is listed on the *Rhone*'s manifest as ship's carpenter. Bert found a piece of the carpenter's skull and leg and rib bones. The grim remains didn't deter Bert from exploring the wreck of the *Rhone* for many years. When Peter Benchley's novel *The Deep* was filmed, Bert served as consultant and diver. The RMS *Rhone* was used as a backdrop for the film. The story involved divers searching for morphine that was part of the ship's cargo. Bert Kilbride, and his great rival on the

John Christopher Fine (red) with Bob and Margaret Weller and Bert Kilbride looking up with a laugh.

islands, George Marler, found many ampoules of morphine among the wreckage of the *Rhone*.

It was the history of the *Rhone* and Benchley's newly acquired scuba diving skills that led to the book after his success with *Jaws*. Bert was the legend that inspired novelist Peter Benchley.

"Bert never threw anything away. After he died, I found an original poster from *The Deep*. It is 6 feet long, the edges were torn and a little rotted. I also found receipts from Columbia Pictures for payments to Bert for his work on the motion picture," Gayla Kilbride related.

"Bert found a place setting for 18 people on the wreckage of the *Rhone*," Gayla said. Happy rivalry existed between the Marlers and Kilbrides. Each offered diving excursions to explore the *Rhone* and other highlights of the BVI. George Marler and his wife Lou were invited to

Saba Rock by Bert for dinner. Bert served them on china from the shipwreck.

George Marler said he would reciprocate the meal and place Bert before a setting marked "second class."

Bert Kilbride (wearing hat) with Bob Weller and shipwreck artifacts.

"He had salt and pepper hair. Wore gold chains around his neck. Bert was a character, fun to be around," Gayla said from her home in St. Petersburg, Florida. The large copper teapot from the *Rhone* forms the base of a coffee table in her living room. The pot itself is filled with hand-blown bottles and bits and pieces of broken china and other artifacts Bert dove up off shipwrecks in the British Virgin Islands.

A painting of the RMS *Rhone* is framed with a rectangular brass fixture from the shipwreck. It graces the portal of Gayla's home. A wood secretary displays Steve Kenyon's skull and a piece of the shirt he was wearing when the *Rhone* sank.

Gayla has been forced to sell many of the *Rhone*'s artifacts. Some were purchased by Sir Richard Branson who bought Moskito Island in the British Virgins. A china plate from the *Rhone* bearing the inscription "Royal Mail Steam Packet Comp." below an ornate royal seal went for $900.

"Bert salvaged a sword handle from an unknown shipwreck that sank off Anegada in the 1700s in 1968," Gayla said. She sold it for $3,950. Many of Bert's Taino pre-Columbian Indian artifacts found on Saba Rock and elsewhere brought high prices. A face pot was sold by Gayla from Bert's collection for $3,150.

Bob Weller had a winning smile. He welcomed divers to his home on "Weller's Cove" and shared tales of high adventure from a lifetime of diving and finding sunken treasure.

Gayla's relationship with Bert Kilbride was no whirlwind affair by any means. She lived in Sun Valley, Idaho and wanted to go sailing. She flew to Tortola to join up with a boat owner "Who turned out to be Captain Blye. I jumped ship," she avers.

"I decided to teach wind surfing. Chip Kilbride, one of Bert's sons, took me to Levrick Bay. Bert came in every day to have French onion soup. I wanted to learn scuba diving. I was 34, Bert was 68, exactly twice my age. He was the youngest 68-year old I ever knew. He did two dives a day, would teach diving in the afternoon and if people wanted to go out he'd take them on a night dive. He had charisma."

In the interim Gayla married another man who eventually went to work for Bert. Gayla left only to be encouraged to return by Bert who was then juggling "His main squeeze, Jackie I. There were two Jackies in his life, Jackie I and Jackie II. Bert and Jackie I had been dating for eighteen years and got along great as long as they were miles apart. If Jackie I was coming back to Saba Rock, Bert would fly me back to the states. He'd time the flights so that I'd leave then he'd pick up Jackie. He only wanted to make one trip to the airport." Gayla has a good sense of humor and her tales of Saba Rock truly set the stage for adventure.

Bert continued to dive the *Rhone* as well as the Royal Navy ship HMS *Astrea*. In 1967, Bert was appointed official Receiver of the Wreck HMS *Astrea*. The thirty-two-gun frigate struck Anegada's reef in 1808. As weather worsened, the captain ordered the *Astrea* abandoned. The ship sank outside the reef. Over years of storms and hurricanes the wreckage was thrown up over the reef and scattered about. Cannons and anchors from the *Astrea* remain in valleys of the reef where musket balls, shot, and brass nails can be seen to this day.

Jackie I knew she was dying of cancer. She wanted to die a Kilbride so Bert and Jackie married in 1986. Gayla and her husband returned to BVI and worked with Bert in his diving operation. "Bert liked my husband. Bert's philosophy was 'provocative maintenance.' My husband could Mickey Mouse engines using bubble gum and bobby pins. Bert fell off the flying bridge of his boat and his son Jimmy left. Bert ended up giving my husband and me Kilbride's Underwater Tours to run."

Eventually Bert sold the business to his oldest son Gary. Gayla ran the office. Tragedy struck Gayla's life when her own son was killed in a motorcycle accident.

"Jackie I died in September and my son died in October. That's what threw Bert and me together. He said Gary needed help doing the book-keeping. I moved back to BVI. Bert said: 'How about committing yourself to Saba Rock?' I asked him, 'Is that your way of proposing?' He answered, 'Why not?'"

Gayla and Bert were married on the 120-foot brigantine Galaxie. Not long thereafter Bert told Gayla he was retiring and she was to run the dive tour business. "The *San Ignacio* was his dream," Gayla said.

They decided to open a bar on Saba Rock. "We'd be having dinner outside and boaters would come by and ask what's for dinner. It was a natural place for a bar. All I had to do was put up a big sign that said BAR. We opened Pirate's Pub. Bert sold Saba Rock in 1996 and we closed the pub in 1997. We did great business. There were two hurricanes one after another, ten days apart," Gayla recounted. The hurricanes devastated new docks they'd installed, sank two of their boats, pushing one right up onto the island and into the guest house.

Gayla had as much as she could bear. Her second son was killed in an automobile accident and their young, adopted son needed attention. Hot water on Saba Rock came from a black garden hose that Bert left out in the sun. At the outset light bulbs were hooked to the 12-volt boat's battery. There were four light bulbs. Only two could be used at a time. Gayla brought a 12-volt television to the island then a generator. More generators were needed for the bar but luxury was never attained on the barren rock. It was, however, a diver's paradise. Reefs beckoned from the doorstep and shipwrecks were everywhere scattered on the reefs and rocks of the British Virgin Islands.

The RMS *Rhone* remains a favorite dive spot off Salt Island in view of Road Town BVI. The water is clear and warm and stories about making of *The Deep* abound. There may not be hand-blown bottles from the stores and cargo, ships' china and brass portholes to be seen, but the wreckage makes a wonderful place to take alluring underwater photographs.

Gayla maintains a representative collection of bottles from the *Rhone* as well as artifacts Bert found underwater over many years diving in the British Virgin Islands. Sentimental treasures from a diver's life. Bert Kilbride loved the legend he created for himself and was content with his self-proclaimed title: "The last pirate of the Caribbean."

"When I die, I want to have my remains placed above Bert's on Neptune Reef. My inscription will be, 'The last pirate's last wench,'" Gayla laughed. An album of photographs was spread open on the glass coffee table top above the *Rhone*'s large tea pot. Treasures from a life of adventure.

BERT KILBRIDE HONORED

Treasure Trove is a little pub tucked away on a corner of Southeast 5th Street in Fort Lauderdale Beach, Florida. The bar was started by a treasure diver that attended a shipwreck symposium begun by Marine Geologist Bill Raymond in Fort Lauderdale in 1984. Just out of college, Ed Stevens met Mel Fisher, Bert Kilbride, and other speakers at the symposium.

The young man began diving with Bert Kilbride on a project to locate a fabled Spanish galleon that sank in the British Virgin Islands. The galleon was never found but plenty of others were located off a 13-mile-long reef that extends from the Island of Anegada between the Atlantic Ocean and Caribbean Sea. It is a treacherous passage even today with modern navigational aids. The shallow reef comes up just below the surface and has claimed ships from time immemorial.

Bert had many wives and as a result many children, grandchildren, and great-grandchildren. His extended family often quips that they are not really sure how many. When they get together to honor their legendary progenitor, the party is fun.

Jeff Rudd took over Treasure Trove bar from his cousin Ed Stevens seventeen years ago. He retained the tradition of the place. His cousin opened Treasure Trove after he worked with treasure salvor Mel Fisher. The British Virgin Islands project had ended. Ed was one of the divers that participated in the amazing finds from the galleon *Nuestra Senora de Atocha*. Ed's idea was to create a bar as tribute to treasure divers and have income to pursue his dream of finding more treasure.

Jeff continued that dream. A two-ton cannon decorated a far wall in front of a window above bottles of liquor. "It was recovered from Muceras Reef, 15 miles north of Cuba," Bill Raymond said. Bill put together a gathering of the Kilbride clan, friends, and divers to dedicate a "chair back."

Bar stools in Treasure Trove carried the names of famous treasure divers. The late Mel Fisher, Burt Webber, Big John McLaughlin, and Chuck Mitchell. Bert was never able to get to Treasure Trove for his chair back dedication so it was done on March 14, 2012, posthumously.

Bert would have been at home among his sons, daughters, grandchildren, and great-grandchildren and the many friends from diving that attended. Gary Kilbride, Bert's oldest son, along with his brother Mike and sister Ellen Kilbride Christopher organized power-point presentations of old films about their diving exploits.

Bert took the 20/20 television film crews of Hugh Downs and Geraldo Rivera underwater to shipwreck sites in the BVI. They raised a canon and anchor. It was at a time during the height of controversy between academicians that wanted shipwrecks left where they were until they could be eventually studied and recovered and treasure hunters that had the investments and means to recover them properly and share the treasure with governments.

Bert had the "look." Beard, darkly-tanned, chiseled face that could have emerged from the pages of Treasure Island as one of its legendary characters. He was the subject of many documentary films, articles, and books. He worked with his sons Gary and Mike and others as well as his last wife Gayla operating Kilbride's Underwater Tours in the BVI.

Everybody recognized Bert's rugged face. He wore a golden Spanish doubloon around his neck on a chain and enjoyed the company of movie stars and best-selling authors like Peter Benchley. Benchley's book, *The Deep*, was scripted into a film made in the British Virgins. It was filmed on the RMS *Rhone*. Of course, Jacqueline Bisset, the film's star, made a great hit with him on Saba Rock especially with her wet T-shirt.

The ornately scripted wood-carved chair back remained at Treasure Trove for patrons to use until the bar's recent closing. The event was commemorated with chicken wings, conch fritters, shrimp and veggie platters prepared by Jeff Rudd and toasted by Bert's friends and family. An occasion for divers with an interest in sunken treasure to get together and for Bert's family and friends to enjoy good fellowship, to share tall tales and true stories about this diving pioneer.

DEEP WATER SHIPWRECKS

The American Civil War dragged on for five years. Battles were waged by young men that prayed to the same God for victory. They spoke the same language and were drawn from all walks of life. The South seceded from the Union. The bombardment of Fort Sumter in Charleston Harbor, South Carolina on April 12, 1861, threw down the cudgel. From the beginning, the end was in sight. A rural, agrarian economy could not long win against industrial might with unlimited resources and troops.

General Robert E. Lee, in command of the Army of Northern Virginia, hoped to push a wedge into the North. It was the South's only hope. If those dissatisfied with war in the North could be convinced it was too costly, then the South could sue for peace on better terms. Peace was the only possible solution and peace would only come if those in power in the North were convinced that the war would not be won easily.

It was a desperate attempt to bring the war into northern homelands that Lee invaded Pennsylvania. The thrust might have succeeded but for the fact that Lee's cavalry commander abandoned his leader at a critical time and made sorties, against orders. Without cavalry, Lee was deprived of his eyes.

The quiet town of Gettysburg became the pivotal point for a three-day battle that saw 51,000 casualties, 8,000 dead. Lee ordered a charge against the Union line on Cemetery Ridge on July 3, 1863. Union forces, behind a stone wall, rained death down upon the advancing lines. Few Confederate troops made it across the field and those that stood at the stone wall were defeated or pushed back.

The war for the South was lost at Gettysburg. Lee retreated with his remaining army into Virginia. The Civil War continued to bleed America for the next two years until Lee's surrender on April 9, 1865, at Appomattox Courthouse in Virginia.

Six months after Lee's surrender, profiteers were taking advantage of the occupied South and its depressed economy. Fortunes were to be made in businesses of all sorts. Defeat of the South meant that its paper money and bank script was worthless as were Confederate bonds. By 1862 the U.S. Treasury issued legal paper money to offset the refusal of merchants to accept state bank paper. No one was exchanging paper money for gold coins and if they did it was at great discount.

Model of the SS *Republic.*

Gold and silver coins were being hoarded. By the summer of 1864, banks that exchanged U.S. treasury-issued paper money required $2,850 for $1,000 in gold. With the California gold rush in 1849, gold became a viable commodity. The coinage act of March 3, 1849, provided for the production of $20 gold coins called double eagles as well as $1 gold coins adding to the circulated $2.50, $5, and $10 denomination gold coins minted in Philadelphia as early as 1795. Ten-dollar gold coins were called eagles. By 1850, golden double eagle $20 gold coins were rolling off mint production lines. Silver dollars were minted in the United States in 1850 and were used as trade dollars overseas. Silver half-dollar coins were scarce but coveted.

There was little gold and silver available in the South after the war. With gold, a person had unlimited purchasing power. It was the era of the carpetbagger. Fortunes were to be made exploiting the relative poverty of the South. Real estate could be bought at depressed prices. Following the devastation of war came a time of rebuilding for America. Material goods and money needed to be pumped into the South and much of the resources to accomplish this were transported by ships. One ship tasked with that mission was the SS *Republic*, recently released from its duties serving the Union navy during the war.

Constructed by John A. Robb in the Fells Point Shipyard in Baltimore in 1853, the SS *Tennessee* was a 1,500-ton, 210-foot-long vessel with a 34-foot-wide beam. The ship had two masts and bowsprit. The hull was made of oak, its decks of white pine fastened with copper and iron. Sails provided auxiliary power to the steam-powered paddlewheels. Coal furnaces fired the boilers that ran a 9-foot long, 6-foot circumference piston. The piston drove a walking beam that was thirty feet long. The walking beam moved up and down and powered a crankshaft that drove twenty-eight-foot paddlewheels mounted on each side of the ship.

The SS *Tennessee* went into service for the Baltimore and Southern Packet Company. The inaugural voyage took place in 1854, when the SS *Tennessee* made a trip with passengers and cargo between Baltimore and Charleston. Although designed for coastal voyages, the ship made one round-trip trans-Atlantic voyage, the first Atlantic crossing by a Baltimore steamship. The *Tennessee* was sold and then began calling on ports in South America and the Caribbean. As traffic to California increased, means were sought to enable passage across Central America. To answer that need, the SS *Tennessee* was briefly used to carry passengers and freight to Nicaragua. Sold once again, the ship was then put on the New York-Havana-New Orleans route for a time, and also between Vera Cruz and New Orleans. Her main trips to Central America were to transport recruits for William Walker's Nicaraguan army, returning to New York in the summer of 1857 with 275 defeated soldiers.

In April 1861, as the Civil War broke out, the ship was impounded by the Confederates while at a wharf in New Orleans. The Rebels hoped to use the ship as a blockade runner. Following Admiral David Farragut's capture of New Orleans on April 25, 1862, the SS *Tennessee* was seized by the Union navy and converted into a powerful gunboat.

Admiral Farragut later made the SS *Tennessee* his flagship for the final months of the Mississippi River Campaign. Following the Battle of Mobile Bay, it was renamed the USS *Mobile* to avoid confusion with the captured Confederate ironclad *Tennessee.*

Damaged in a storm in the Gulf of Mexico in 1864, the ship was sent to the Brooklyn Navy Yard for repairs. It was decommissioned in December 1864, then sold for $25,000 in March of 1865, and christened the SS *Republic.* The ship was put into service between New York and New Orleans. It made four round trips carrying passengers and freight.

On her fifth voyage on October 18, 1865, the SS *Republic* departed New York with eighty passengers and crew and an enormous cargo of goods including barrels of money bound to help fuel the South's expanding post-Civil War economy. The ship's holds were swollen with crates of bottles of champagne and wines, pickled foodstuffs, religious porcelains and glassware, as well as cloth and other items essential to life in mid-nineteenth-century America.

Hurricane force winds struck the paddlewheel steamer in the Atlantic on October 23. Valiant efforts by crew and passengers to lighten the ship, to pump and bail water failed. The SS *Republic* sank at 4 PM on October 25, 1865. Four lifeboats and a make-shift raft were launched putting survivors at peril in a storm-tossed ocean. They watched the vessel slip under the waves with a fortune in silver and gold aboard.

All of the passengers and crew abandoned ship during the sinking of the *Republic*. At least one poor soul never made it through the ship's scattered debris. Most of those that scrambled aboard a hastily made raft of spars and wood succumbed. Only one or two of the 14–18 on the raft were saved when it was found drifting off Cape Hatteras, 300 miles from where the *Republic* sank. The four lifeboats were picked up by passing vessels and the survivors brought into Charleston, Hilton Head, and Port Royal. The *Republic* sank in the Atlantic about 100 miles off the Georgia coast in 1,700 feet of water.

In 1994 industry pioneer Greg Stemm co-founded a company to explore the deep oceans with modern technology. Remotely operated vehicles (ROVs) had been used to inspect underwater cables and pipelines and for military purposes. Great successes were had with the discovery of deep-water shipwrecks like the *Titanic* and Central America. Deep-water exploration and recovery technology existed but was costly.

Odyssey Marine Exploration was formed to plumb the deep oceans with the knowledge that divers and contemporary salvors worked over shallow water shipwrecks but there weren't any groups with the investment in technology, specialists, and research to consistently explore shipwrecks in greater depths. From past experience in deep-ocean shipwreck exploration, the Odyssey team was convinced that with their tools and expertise, they could locate ships like the SS *Republic* and other shipwrecks of interest over many miles of ocean. The wreck of the *Republic* was only a speck in a vast area to search despite reports made by survivors and the captain and crew of the vessel's probable location when it sank in the hurricane.

As their research progressed in May 2002, the explorers began to search for the SS *Republic* in earnest, having defined a large search area off the coast of Georgia. They subsequently purchased one of the world's most renowned research vessels and equipped it as a search boat with sophisticated side-scan sonar.

Within the year they would locate what a crew member first dismissed as a "sailboat" underwater. Persistence paid off. On August 2, 2003, images of the "sailboat" recorded on deep-water video cameras showed the wreckage to be a sidewheel paddle steamer. Ten days later a U.S. District Admiralty Court confirmed that Odyssey was the salvor in possession of the shipwreck.

It wasn't until October 9, 2003, that the company's ROV ZEUS, on its tether from the support ship, 1,700 feet above, located the ship's bell, proof positive from the remaining inscription on the recovered bell that it belonged to the SS *Tennessee*. The SS *Republic* was found. Within months a fortune in American gold coins, silver half-dollars, and bountiful amounts of general cargo–a plethora of artifacts reminiscent of life in the mid-nineteenth century was discovered.

Ship's bell of the SS *Republic* in conservation bath at Odyssey Marine headquarters lab in Tampa, Florida.

Sophisticated manipulator arms on the ROV along with a blower that can push sand away and a suction cup device that acts

Ellen Gerth with bottles recovered from the wreck of the SS *Republic* being conserved.

Ink bottle recovered from the wreck of the SS *Republic*.

Odyssey Marine's conservator Ellen Gerth with delicate porcelain ornaments recovered from the cargo of the wrecked SS *Republic*.

like a limpet to pick up individual objects enabled the salvors to raise artifacts and coins off the scattered wreckage.

The team consisted of archaeologists and experts in almost every field of shipwreck exploration. Detailed photographic surveys were made of the sunken ship in situ. Photographs and videos were taken of every element of the vessel and its debris. The entire archaeological excavation was captured on video and documented in the company's proprietary DataLog™ system.

The SS *Republic* had broken apart and spilled its cargo in the form of a giant watermelon. Decks had collapsed. Boilers, the walking beam, the great paddle wheels, remains of the ship itself were captured on high-definition video. What the Odyssey team found was a time capsule preserved almost intact. The 14,000 artifacts recovered from the site by Odyssey were from a period in time just months following the end of the American Civil War.

"We conserve these artifacts in our land-based facility, and the conservation of many of these objects continues today," Ellen Gerth said, speaking from the company's modern, state-of-the-art conservation laboratory in Tampa, Florida.

A specialist in cultural heritage management and the care and research of collections, Gerth is Odyssey's Archaeological Curator of Collections. "Our work entails conservation, documentation and the exhibition of artifacts, and we actively present our shipwreck discoveries in archaeological

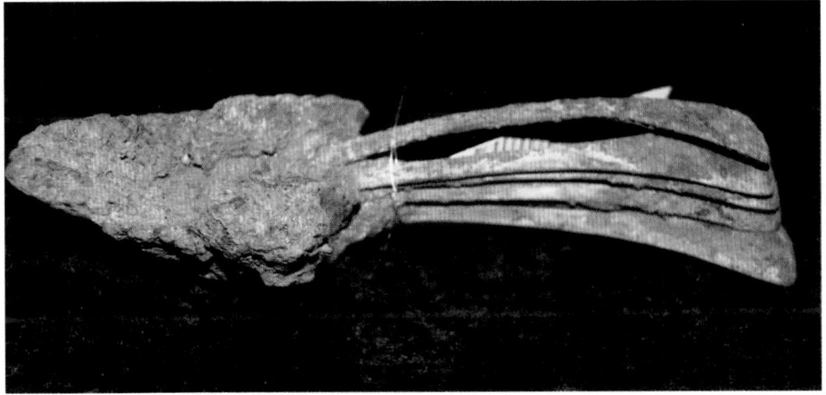

Eight spoons fused together recovered from the sunken remains of the SS *Republic*.

Clump of coins recovered from the extreme depths where the wreck of the SS *Republic* lies.

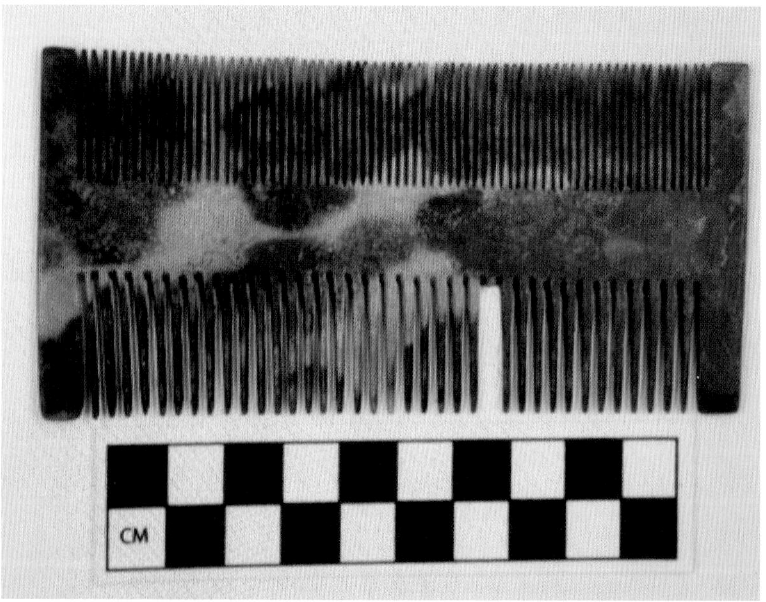

A delicate comb with fine tines used to remove lice from infected hair brought up intact from the deep water wreck of the SS *Republic* and perfectly preserved in their conservation laboratory.

Clump of coins recovered from the wreck of the SS *Republic*.

Odyssey Marine's president Mark Gordon with gold coins from the SS *Republic* on display in Odyssey's offices in Tampa, Florida.

papers published on our website and in our Oceans Odyssey archaeological volumes. We also support educational outreach, which includes curriculum to accompany our traveling shipwreck exhibit. From the start, we have understood that you can't do archaeology without a commitment to the highest standards in conservation. Often archaeologists have no control over the movement of artifacts following excavation, and sometimes they have no interest in the artifacts after their work is done, in which case they don't always publish their findings. Disseminating the information and knowledge we glean from our shipwreck excavation projects is especially important and vital to our mission," she explained.

"In some countries there is no follow up. There are two different worlds: archaeology and conservation. We've tied these together," John Oppermann, Odyssey's Director of Archaeology, Research and Conservation added. Teamwork between researchers, ROV operators, archaeologists, project managers, conservators and curators made possible the process of finding the SS *Republic*, documenting the shipwreck, bringing artifacts to the surface, and identifying and conserving them in a seamless, carefully managed fashion. The result of Odyssey's work is a model with several avenues in which to share the invaluable knowledge provided by shipwreck exploration and research. The company has discovered a vast variety of thousands of artifacts that help piece together forgotten history.

"One of the most intriguing aspects of what we do is learning about the artifacts and the role they played in pivotal events in history. For example, on the SS *Republic*, we recovered 96 religious artifacts including pressed glass crucifix candlesticks, and holy water fonts and angels. It is an assemblage that was intended to be sold in New Orleans, a city torn by war and seeking comfort in religion as it struggled to rebuild," Oppermann said as he described a collection of glass and porcelain religious statues and crosses on display in the conservation lab.

"It is unlikely that these religious items were going to a church. A church would typically have bigger, more elaborate statues. People set up holy corners in their homes. These artifacts were discovered in 2004, yet the research continued for years. We were not able to discern the French origins of the porcelain until 2009. I found a porcelain expert that pulled it together," Gerth said.

"It makes it really exciting to find people with expertise that want to identify artifacts and share their knowledge," she added. The glass crucifixes were produced by the Boston & Sandwich Glass Company in Massachusetts.

Of great interest to Odyssey are the stories of the people aboard the shipwrecks they discover, including the SS *Republic*. Especially rewarding is being able to share the information uncovered through its exploration and research with the descendants of the passengers. One such passenger, a former Union Colonel with a Vermont Regiment, embarked with his brother to make their fortune in the impoverished South. Colonel William T. Nichols survived the Battle of Gettysburg and survived in a lifeboat with his brother Henry after the fatal sinking of the SS *Republic*. Thirst was so severe that Nichols put the chain of a locket that contained a photograph of his wife in his mouth. His brother sucked on a coin.

One of Odyssey's researchers found and contacted the Nichols family. The very locket survived the ordeal and was in the possession of Colonel Nichols' great-great granddaughter whom the Odyssey team had the honor of meeting.

"To see the actual locket that he used to ease his distress from thirst was exciting. Colonel Nichols had been keeping a journal. When he got safely to land, he sent his wife a letter describing the events aboard ship and after the sinking. The couple had lost their daughter May to typhoid fever before Nichols left on the voyage. His wife Thyrza received Nichols' letter just before she too died of the fever. Colonel Nichols went on to become a prosperous businessman and founded a town in Illinois he called Maywood, named for the daughter he lost," Gerth related.

Research and documentation aren't just conducted topside. From the start, shipwreck sites undergo a pre-disturbance survey so that archaeologists can go back and study the site as it was prior to excavation.

"The SS *Republic* site required 2,500 individual photographs to put together this accurate portrayal of the shipwreck on the ocean bottom. The final product is a photomosaic which provides the archaeologists a tool they can use topside to plan and direct excavation strategies so as not to damage the site as artifacts are recovered. Odyssey's photomosaic technology has improved since the discovery of the SS *Republic*; the process is a lot more efficient with the improving technology," Oppermann explained.

"Most importantly, we adhere to the highest standards in deep-ocean marine archaeology, a field which to a large extent is still in its infancy," Oppermann added.

Odyssey recovered more than 51,000 coins from the SS *Republic*, a quarter of the coins reportedly aboard the vessel when it sank. The yearlong archaeological excavation recovered more than 14,000 artifacts from the sea floor including 8,000 glass and stoneware bottles containing foodstuffs, spirits, hair tonics, and patent medicines. In many cases the contents of the bottles remained intact, preserved in the cold water of the ocean depths.

"Researchers at Florida State University tested some of the bottles we recovered from the SS *Republic*. They found some microbial growth but interestingly, not a lot of salinity. Preservation processes in 1865 appear to have been pretty good," Gerth reported.

Conservation Technician Alan Bosel held up a cathedral pepper sauce bottle, a uniquely decorative bottle that contained its original contents. "These are red and yellow peppers. The hot flavor was often used to disguise unpleasant tastes. In those days meat was not always fresh. Unlike today where spices are used to enhance flavor, pepper sauce helped mask the taste of unsavory foods," Bosel said.

A variety of artifacts from everyday life were brought to the surface and conserved in Odyssey's lab, bone toothbrushes, hair combs, game pieces, spoons, and leather shoes. Also recovered were portholes and of course, the ship's bell. The coins aboard had been packed in coarse sacking, then placed into wooden barrels, most of which eventually disintegrated in the saltwater environment, leaving the coins exposed to the elements.

Lying on the Atlantic seabed for well over a century, many of the coins concreted together, resulting in a solid mass of coins combined with seabed sediments, minerals, and organic matter. "We recovered a number of large coin clumps in varying sizes." Gerth opened a bin filled with water and chemicals that contained one example comprised of silver Seated Liberty half-dollars. "You can actually see the remnants of the canvas bag in which the coins were packed and the remains of the wooden keg. The coin concretion will remain in conservation until all of the salts are removed; it may then make for an intriguing exhibit piece."

To many people, shipwreck exploration can seem like a whimsical adventure and not a viable career choice. Years before Odyssey was created, Mark Gordon, a shipwreck dive enthusiast who held an MBA in finance, devised a business plan for a company to explore the deep ocean. Through serendipitous events, Mark was introduced to Greg Stemm, who was establishing such a company. The two kept in regular contact through the years. In 2003, as Odyssey was equipping its newly purchased archaeological platform, the *Odyssey Explorer*, Greg called on Mark to help.

"I had just sold my company to the Rockefeller Group in New York when Greg called me in September 2003 as Odyssey was outfitting their research and exploration vessel in Baltimore. He asked whether I had ever put technology systems on a boat."

"Two weeks after becoming the President of a Rockefeller Company, I was helping Greg pull cables through the *Odyssey Explorer*. This opportunity led me back to my true passion and allowed me the opportunity to participate in the business that I envisioned in the business plan that I had formulated in my MBA program years before," Mark Gordon, Odyssey's President and Chief Operating Officer said.

Mark's expertise in building successful businesses would help Odyssey during its transition from a group that set out to find shipwrecks into a company that is publicly traded on the NASDAQ stock exchange, employs hundreds of professionals and is now known as the world leader in deep ocean exploration with several key shipwreck discoveries announced since 2003's *Republic* discovery.

"It is expensive to work in the deep ocean. We spend on average $2½ million a month running our operations when the ships are on the water working. Marine operations are our largest expense. We've successfully stayed funded for over 18 years and we are fortunate to have assembled a team of individuals who are deeply committed to the mission of discovering and learning from historic shipwrecks," Gordon said.

"It's not just the stories of the artifacts and people that are contained in shipwrecks. There are many ways in which deep-ocean research can be of benefit. We submitted biological samples to a hospital research program and they have isolated a protein that appears to be a form of antibiotic that is effective against six of seven known forms of antibiotic-resistant Staphylococcus infections. We've donated hundreds of hours of video to Florida State University so they can study a rare shark. It costs us $50,000 to $100,000 a day to work on site . . . we can give practical experience with proper standards and share our knowledge . . . knowledge really matters. We have an exhibit about our deep-ocean exploration that has been on display at science centers and museums around the country. Over one million people have visited the exhibit already. Kids learn from the hands-on elements featured in the exhibit that make learning fun for them. We also have a virtual museum on the web. Odyssey'sVirtualMuseum.com is accessible to anyone, for free, at any time," Gordon explained.

The SS *Republic* opened a window on the world after the Civil War, with its bottled foodstuffs and patent medicines, its tools, glassware, and other items of trade. The fortune of gold and silver coins is estimated to be valued at $75 million. Some 4,135 gold coins were recovered. Of these, there were 2,675 double eagles, and 1,460 eagles and some 47,263 silver coins, but what might have been the most intriguing coin is a Liberty Seated Silver half dollar inscribed with the word "WAR," a proclamation that mirrored the sentiment of a nation divided.

More than the wealth aboard was the history and human stories behind the history. The SS *Republic* spanned an age of Civil War and reconstruction. Its recovery saved history lost under the ocean. The persistence and courage of men of vision, then and now, brought about America's greatness and lasting legacy in times of trial and times of healing. The discovery and excavation of the SS *Republic* offers insight into a slice of life now preserved forever.

TREASURE OF THE AZTEC CRYSTAL SKULLS

He holds degrees from McGill University in Canada, created a website that is visited by millions of people that documents religion, is a marine archaeologist and art connoisseur. Powerfully built with an intellect that finds interest in any subject, Dr. Victor Benilous has found shipwrecks containing important artifacts from the Spanish colonial period off Florida's shores. His profile fits the fictional character Indiana Jones although this West Palm Beach resident is quick to admit he enjoys the movies but relies on painstaking research to find sunken treasure.

From their Mizner home in a historic district in West Palm, Vic, with his wife Sue and a team of trusted colleagues, has ventured around the world in quest of treasure. In some cases, they have turned up priceless art treasures hidden by Facists during World War II, in others explored and reported on one of the earliest shipwrecks found in the Western Hemisphere.

"The shipwreck dates from the early 1500s. There was no treasure aboard. We found many pieces of pottery and some artifacts but no gold or silver," Vic explained. The wreck, located off Juno Beach, Florida, provided the team with important evidence of Spanish shipbuilding and colonial life.

From the experience gained during the exploration of the Juno wreck, Dr. Benilous and his team were called upon to try and locate a ship that sank in deep waters of the Atlantic somewhere off Cape Canaveral. The

John Christopher Fine (wearing dive hood), holding clump of uncut emerald crystals with Dr. Victor Benilous with silver bar and gold splash.

wreck contained important artifacts and treasures said taken by Hernan Cortez from the Aztecs during his conquest of Mexico.

"Cortez remarried. He had gone back to Spain and was enmeshed in controversy with the Royal family over the treasures he obtained. He eventually received favor once the truth about his discoveries was explained. A valiant warrior and cruel exploiter of the indigenous people, Cortez amassed a personal fortune. Gold and silver artifacts taken from the Aztecs were often melted into ingots of bullion and shipped back to Spain. The King obtained a "quinto" or a fifth, as the Royal share of all specie and goods obtained in the New World. Cortez paid the Royal "quinto" and had much treasure left over as his personal spoils.

"Some 250 years after Cortez' death part of his fortune still remained in Mexico. It was being shipped back to Spain. Somewhere off the Atlantic coast of Florida a captain reported seeing smoke on the horizon. The location of the ship that apparently burned to the water line and sank was very vague," Dr. Benilous said.

Finding something in the ocean, even with precise coordinates, can be difficult. Finding a shipwreck in very deep water with only a vague idea of its location is often impossible. Dr. Benilous was engaged by members of the family of the second wife of Cortez. They had some information about the shipwreck and the cargo it carried. The treasure was to be used in Spain by the family to obtain land grants in Mexico.

"I used psychics before. The same psychics that are hired by the U.S. government and used by police to find missing persons. These people have a special gift. I sent two maps with plastic overlays to each of two well-known psychics. The maps came back marked almost within the same ocean area. This was phenomenal. It still meant that there was an immense ocean to cover. We had to narrow down the search area," Dr. Benilous said.

They engaged the services of one of the psychics. He was taken aboard the team's research vessel. "It was mind boggling. We got to a place where the location had been marked on the map. As we navigated the area the psychic said, 'Dive here.'"

Dr. Benilous put a diver in the water. "On that first dive, not ten feet from where the psychic said 'dive,' we found the first of our Aztec crystal skulls."

Divers underwater with emerald crystals and gold cross.

The discovery was made in 1993, long before Indiana Jones had any notion of the mystery of the crystal skulls. The discovery was reported in the press and eventually formed a *Time Magazine* cover story. As the Mayan calendar approached 2012, interest perked about predictions for world change they foresaw. Much revolved around thirteen large crystal skulls that, if united, would hold the knowledge of the universe.

Dr. Benilous began diving and recovery operations in deep international waters. "We tried to keep a low profile. When we suspected boats were following us to get the position of the wreck, we simply engaged in a day of fishing."

"The crystal skull is a magnificent example. When we found the first one, very few were known to exist in the world. One is in the London Museum. That one is life size. Another is in private hands found in a Mayan excavation in what is now Belize," Sue Benilous explained.

Artifacts were raised in large clumps. Divers found charred remains of wood, proving that the ship had indeed burned to the water line as the captain of yore reported. Many fine pre-Colombian Aztec objects were recovered along with treasure. Some of the most interesting objects recovered were three perfectly formed crystal skulls.

"There are no modern tool marks on these crystal skulls. As far as modern research goes the Mayans did not have the technology to produce such perfect crystal skulls. Crystal is very hard. It is difficult to work. Using modern technology to carve crystal, a skull will bear marks that can be seen under a microscope. These crystal skulls have no tool marks," Dr. Benilous said.

The Mitchell-Hedges crystal skull, from a Mayan temple in Lubantuum, Belize, is clear crystal. It is the size of a human skull. The bottom jaw was made from the same piece of crystal and is detachable. This is an amazing feat. The Mitchell-Hedges crystal skull is one of the world's most startling archaeological discoveries made in the 1920s. The Benilous team's discoveries of smaller crystal skulls from a Spanish colonial shipwreck, with provenance to the time of conquest, proved early Aztecs and Mayans possessed these crystal skulls. Did they make them themselves or were they something they obtained from earlier cultures?

"Did the conquistadors destroy information that may have given evidence of early people's ability to create such fine work?" The mystery of the crystal skulls is not solved. What is apparent is that Dr. Benilous and his team have determined to preserve the artifacts intact and to present them as an exhibit that will also detail the history of conquest of the New World.

The Cortez Project is ongoing. The group will not disclose the location of the shipwreck. Its remote Atlantic Ocean location would leave it open to pillage by treasure seekers they aver. Over time the intrepid explorers have been recovering artifacts and preserving them.

"We plan a major exhibit. Imagine having a recreation of a treasure galleon here in Palm Beach. Inside would be a theatre with holograms that describes the history of conquest. It would trace the route of Cortez in Mexico. There would be a treasure room where people could explore and partake of history. Our research will be made available for all to share. It is not a matter of trying to sell artifacts. We are keeping the collection together and are in discussion with organizations that have an interest in creating a display that will enable us to share this knowledge with the world," Dr. Benilous said.

There is a real Indiana Jones. He is working on preserving the marine archaeology of important Aztec artifacts recovered from the deep ocean. His exploits are legendary and comply with high ideals for the preservation of knowledge that otherwise would be lost forever. The mystery is real and the adventure continues. Treasures stolen from exploited peoples in the Americas may help focus attention on the Mayan legacy. Crystals, after all, are what we use to store knowledge and transmit information.

"The first radio used a crystal. Computers use crystal chips," Dr. Benilous said. "Is it just that we don't know how to extract the knowledge from this crystal skull?" He asked, holding the object in his hands, contemplating the important role the shipwreck will play in promoting human understanding.

GIVING BACK

Palm Beach County Ocean Lifeguard Lieutenant Peter Leo was told about an anchor located near the public bathing beach. He snorkeled out and saw a large ship's anchor in about twenty feet of water. The anchor had an intact wooden stock and intact iron flukes. It was completely uncovered, lying in the sand.

Peter Leo's new exploit pales in comparison with his discovery of the Spanish aviso or courier ship off Jupiter Beach years before when he worked with the State of Florida and archaeologists to explore and excavate finds from what has been identified as *San Miguel Archangel.* Artifacts from that shipwreck are on display at the Loxahatchee Historical Society Museum in Jupiter and in the Museum of Florida History in Tallahassee.

Two cannons and an anchor from the *San Miguel* shipwreck are preserved in a park on grounds of the Loxahatchee Historical Society Museum at Jupiter Lighthouse. Two more cannons and another anchor from the *San Miguel* have been donated to Palm Beach County and are on display at Jupiter Inlet Park. While Peter Leo's latest find is evidently from a more recent shipwreck, an iron hulled sailing vessel of 1890s vintage, it is still an important piece of history.

"A snorkeler found the anchor in July 2009. It was very exposed. He contacted Brian Portman, a diver that installs underwater moorings and does salvage work. Brian contacted me." Leo described his first contacts about the anchor.

Peter snorkeled out from the beach after work and examined the anchor. The next day he came down to the site by skiff and met Brian Portman. They snorkeled the site, found the anchor completely exposed and placed a tag on it.

Leo contacted State of Florida authorities and advised them of the find. When Leo and Portman returned the next day, the anchor had been

Peter Leo with preserved cannons and anchor recovered from the Jupiter shipwreck prior to their placement at Lighthouse Park in Jupiter, Florida.

moved. "Somebody tried to steal it. A person in the condo opposite told us that he saw a boat on the site during the night. We decided we had to raise the anchor to protect it," Leo explained. He took pictures of the anchor on the ocean floor.

Brian Portman had commercial lift bags from his business. The divers attached them to the anchor underwater. "There was an incredible lightning storm and thunder. My sister was on the boat with me. She was terrified. Never experienced a lightning storm like this. We could see lightning flashes underwater and heard thunderclaps."

With lift bags in place, the anchor was raised off the bottom. "It weighed a thousand pounds. We towed it slowly north, three feet beneath the surface with the lift bags attached. Got it through the Jupiter Inlet. We dropped it in front of the old Coast Guard dock at the Jupiter lighthouse."

Peter Leo contacted the State of Florida, Department of State, Division of Historical Resources in Tallahassee. He spoke with the Chief Archaeologist Dan McClanon and informed him that they had an intact anchor.

"We arranged a meeting. State Archaeologist James Levy came down with a government flatbed truck. I enlisted the help of Captain Jack Pope, owner of a jack up barge the Polly L. The barge was used excavating the Jupiter Wreck. Captain Pope volunteered and brought the barge in. He used a crane to lift the anchor onto the state's truck," Leo explained.

The anchor was conserved in the state laboratory. The wooden stock was preserved and the iron stabilized so that salt crystals do no cause it to crumble and break apart once exposed to air.

Anchors and cannons from the Jupiter shipwreck have been returned on loan to a local museum and placed on display at the Lighthouse Museum and Loxahatchee Historical Society as well as in DuBois Park where they can be enjoyed by everyone.

"Anchors were switched around on ships. They were not always original equipment on board. This was clearly a large iron hulled sailing vessel that wrecked on shore," Leo said. He is continuing his research to determine the origin on the shipwreck and to help the State identify the vessel that wrecked off Riviera Beach.

KEYS TREASURE

Both men spanned an era of exploration and discovery in the Florida Keys. They learned by doing, trial and error; both had a wealth of experience searching the ocean for the remains of Spanish galleons that wrecked in the fury of a hurricane in 1733. Gordon Cottrell built his aluminum boat from the hull up. Everything aboard was designed to make the work boat *C-Arc* practical for supporting divers and the equipment they needed to search the sandy bottom where treasure might be found.

Burt Webber startled the world when he discovered the treasure galleon *Concepcion* that wrecked on the Silver Banks north of the Dominican Republic in 1641. Burt found the remains of the *Concepcion* in 1978. Movies were made about his exploits and *National Geographic* described his adventure.

Burt was in Tavernier aboard Gordy's boat running tests on new and sophisticated cesium magnetometers. Both men were skilled engineers. Gordy spent much of his career in Wisconsin reviewing engineering blueprints before meeting his wife in Florida and moving to Key Largo

David Foster (beard) with Mick O'Connor searching for a Spanish galleon off Florida's coast.

Burt Webber (hand on his hip) and his project manager examining arms they stow aboard to protect from piracy on the high seas during recovery operations.

John Christopher Fine with Burt Webber (hat) discussing state-of-the-art magnetometer to be used in upcoming treasure recovery project.

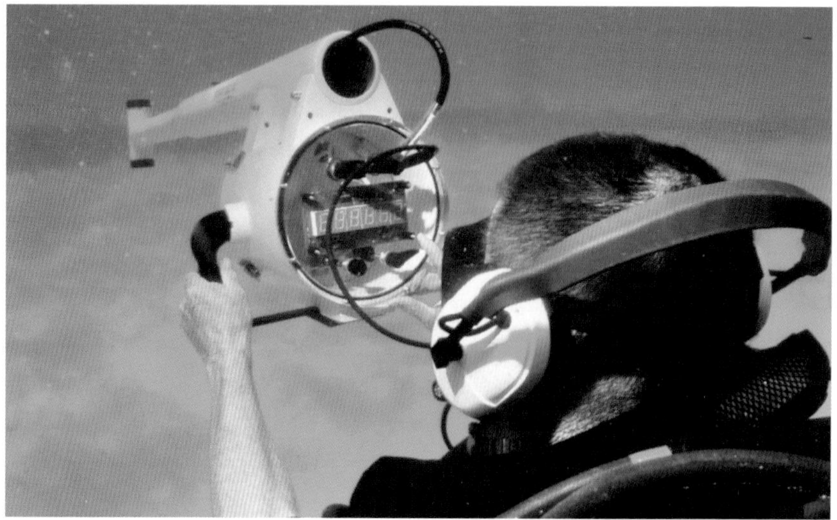

Burt Webber with new state-of-the-art magnetometer he helped develop, testing it in the Atlantic Ocean off the Florida Keys.

where he operated his own welding business. Burt has always been a diver and ocean explorer that conceived new equipment, designed and perfected existing technology to find treasure underwater.

C-Arc's crew was made up of diver Lawrence Campbell, a cannon founder and owner of Campbell Cannon and Carriage Works. He makes reproduction cannons and carriages out of bronze and has a great interest in historic cannons from Spanish galleons. Webber was joined by his 38-year-old son Kurt and members of his crew, Greg Erkes, Brian Barnes and Captain Shannon Wilkins. They brought cesium magnetometers that Burt designed and needed to test before the Webber team would embark on a six-month voyage to the Dominican Republic to search for treasure.

Gordy had to time his departure from Tavernier Creek to coincide with the tides since the sandy bottom is not deep. The plan was to tow one magnetometer on a cable behind the boat and mark "hits or places that gave a reading." The next day they would return to the sites and go in the water with handheld magnetometers to dive on the hits and pinpoint them.

"I've been diving out here for years. The last guy that had the contract on the *Capitana* was Don Washington. I got the contract from Don . . . I work it in conjunction with the Florida Keys National Marine Sanctuary," Gordy said.

Burt Webber suited up for a dive.

The *Capitana*, officially called *El Rubi Segundo*, commanded by General Don Rodrigo de Torres y Morales, sailed out of Havana Harbor on July 13, 1733, with a fleet of treasure galleons. The ship is called the *Capitana* because it was the flagship of the convoy, the lead ship. Two days later the convoy was caught in a furious hurricane and the ships were dashed upon the shallow sand banks and reefs of the Florida Keys.

El Rubi, the *Capitana*, was sunk in a place not far from the location of Davis Light almost straight out from Tavernier Inlet. The shipwreck was worked by pioneer diver Ark McKee, then by Bob Weller and others. It is a difficult place to work. The Keys sanctuary is a protected area and Gordy must ensure that he does not damage grass beds or other natural resources when he uses air lifts or the mailbox that he can mount over the stern of his vessel. The mailbox would enable Gordy to blow away heavy overburden of sand covering the wreckage but also causes that blown sand to drift for a time before settling.

The area of the *Capitana* ballast pile is in a sandy stretch of ocean a long way from the ocean reef situated much further out. There are grass beds that must be protected although the vast area is mostly barren sand. The men did not work airlifts underwater, the team was focused on testing the equipment.

"My training ground was out here. I love it. I used to charter a boat from Captain Bill Fox before I got the air-sea rescue ship we used. We'd track the ten-fathom line. I thought the *Atocha* was there. Everybody was in a learning process. All the keys were called Matecumbe. Wc were looking for the last key of the Matecumbe. Here's where I first met Mel Fisher and Fay Feild. Fisher was working upper Key Largo. He thought the *Atocha* had wrecked on the last key. It wasn't until researcher Gene Lyon found the archive record that said 'Los Marques,' that Fisher went to Key West," Burt Webber said.

"I haven't made a dive since last Thanksgiving. That was a high-tech dive on the Captain Kidd wreck in eight feet of water," he laughed.

"If the government would let us do our job, they would have more treasure than they'd know what to do with . . . archaeologists label us rapists. I have an archaeologist on my team. I don't mind working with them," Gordy Cottrell said.

He was working within the guidelines and restrictions placed upon him by the sanctuary and State of Florida. He welcomed Webber and his team's use of high-tech underwater diver held cesium magnetometers. Each handheld unit cost $36,000 and there were only two in existence. Webber owned them both. Being able to pinpoint wreckage under the sand was critical.

Centuries after the *Capitana*'s wrecking nothing was visible underwater. Even the ballast pile, river rocks that had been set in the ship to give it stability and weight as it sailed, were now under sand. The wooden members of the ship had long since been either cast away by storms, waves, and hurricanes or eaten by sea worms. If any wood remained, it would only be preserved under deep sand.

They didn't find treasure on this trip. Burt Webber found that his equipment worked but he needed to engineer minor adjustments to make the units comfortable for his divers since the probes tended to sink forward and put a strain on their wrists over time. Set screws needed to be refined. Gordy Cottrell received the results of the magnetometer surveys and would come back to explore the hits at a later time.

"Yes, it looks like the *Capitana* struck there and may have been pushed in that direction," Gordy said as he examined bright orange painted surface markers the divers threw in. Time would tell whether new history under the sea would be found and shared with the world.

The lure of sunken treasure, tales of pirates, and daring-do fire every person's imagination, young or old. Legendary divers like Burt Webber have fired the imaginations of new generations of ocean explorers. Burt Webber and the late Gordy Cottrell have followed their dreams and, as a result, have been able to share their discoveries and knowledge with the world.

YOU CAN NEVER FIND IT ALL

Despite the fact that sites offshore of the beaches between Fort Pierce and Sebastian, Florida have been worked for many years, treasure still turns up. A mother-daughter team, Bonnie and Jo Schubert, dive the shipwrecks off Fort Pierce every season under sub-contract with the permittee. In 2010 Bonnie found a gold statue. The object is a Catholic religious ornament thought to be of a pelican mother revitalizing her offspring with her own blood. Symbolic allegory of Jesus' death on the cross. While estimates of value for the 5½" statue are variously given, some expect it to bring almost $1 million when it is eventually sold at auction.

Bonnie made her find in shallow water just offshore of Frederick Douglas Beach. It was here that I detected, but couldn't recover, signals in the sand at water's edge long ago. A friend returned to the same beach and found a rare Guatemala fully dated silver "Ocho Reales" or Piece of Eight that was estimated to be worth $2,500. Proof again that a site is never fully exploited, especially underwater and on beaches that change with storms and wave action.

Another veteran diver, John Brandon, directed operations on the 1715 treasure fleet site for many years. Despite bad weather Brandon would be on site with his boat digging holes. He and his team usually led recovery efforts and most often ended the season with some of the best finds.

Brandon knew that coins turned up on the beaches after every hurricane. When a major storm threatened, he got in his truck and drove to a relative's house on a peninsula. He knew that all residents would be evacuated because of the impending storm and that access to the area would be cut off by authorities for days following the hurricane to prevent looting.

He drove into the driveway just as the family were driving out with possessions they wanted to protect. He was warned of the danger but determined that he would brave out the hurricane in his truck and be in place when the storm subsided to comb the beach with his metal detector.

Hurricane force winds and wild ocean waves came ashore on Florida's Atlantic coast. Brandon hunkered down in his truck. A large tree toppled over near him but did not fall on his truck. By morning the storm passed over and Brandon got out his metal detector. He made it across the street through rubble and down to the beach. Devastation was everywhere.

The Atlantic Ocean roiled. Rollers continued to throw debris up on the beach already littered with wreckage and whole downed trees. Brandon's path was blocked by debris so he slipped into the ocean to get past obstacles. A large wave sent him crashing into the trunk of an uprooted tree. Pain shot through his body. He moved on and was able to regain the beach with his metal detector unharmed.

Sweeping the sand, Brandon began getting hits. Within an hour he found nine gold coins. They had been tossed up from offshore wreckage. It was as it had been in the days Kip Wagner walked the beach after storms so long ago and picked Spanish colonial coins from the sand.

CONFIRMED BEACH DETECTORISTS

Bill Cassinelli and Hank Haart both worked as divers on the Weller team. Their passion is detecting beaches in line with where Spanish ships were wrecked in hurricanes. Their skill with detectors is legend but their perseverance has made them successful finding coins.

Both detected along the narrow strip called Treasure Beach near Lower Matecumbe Key at Mile Marker 74 in the Florida Keys. It was offshore of this spit of land that the Spanish nao *San Felipe* also called *El Lerri* grounded and wrecked during the 1733 hurricane. Over time wreckage was scattered by ocean storms and hurricanes. This is the spot where many years before tourists surprised Weller and his pals when they were directed to the beach and found Spanish relics and coins. It is where Brad Williamson found his magnificent gold and emerald pendant.

On one trip Hank discovered some modern coins and what appeared to be a Spanish coin that had been rubbed blank by the elements. The

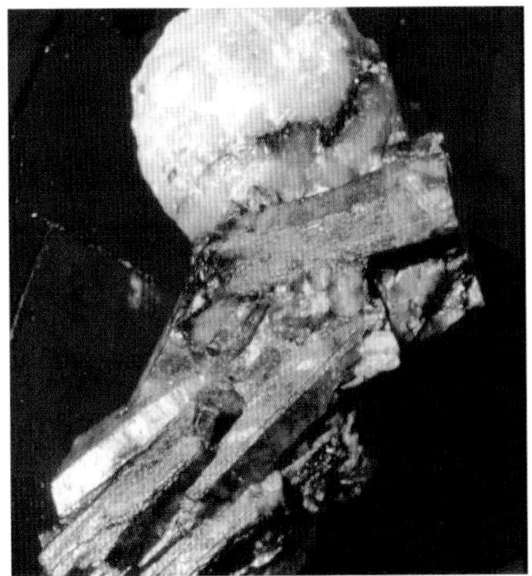

Emerald crystals weighing 25,000 carats in a quartz matrix.

Aztec crystal skulls, crystals of emerald including a 964-carat six-sided crystal, and gold Aztec adornment.

Emeralds were valued by the Spanish Conquistadors. They shunned jade, the stone valued above all else by indigenous peoples of the lands they exploited. Emeralds, cut and uncut, from the cargo of a Spanish ship wrecked off Florida's coast.

Divers Hank Haart (sunglasses) and Bill Cassinelli with rare Spanish minted pieces of eight that Bill found on Treasure Beach. They are dated 1732, the first year that a screw press was used to mint coins in the New World.

discoveries enticed Bill to take the drive down to the Keys from his home in St. Lucie, Florida near the beaches where the 1715 fleet wrecked.

"I got a hit and found a round clump," Bill Cassinelli told the story. He picked the clump up and put it in his bag. Corrosion and concretions surrounded the little clump but it gave a hit for conductive metal.

"When I broke the clump apart there were two newly minted 1732 pillar dollars inside. The sides that faced each other were perfect, just as they came from the mint. The outside, exposed to the ocean and elements, was corroded. If the coins had been perfect, they would be worth $10,000 each," Bill said. Proof again that even at a site where others have looked before, there is still treasure to be found. Like other legends in treasure diving, Bill passed over the bar.

CARTOGRAPHY OF SUNKEN TREASURE

Long before satellites, before cameras in space could zoom in on every house, when computers were DaVinci's dream, before the typewriter was the ultimate writing machine, maps were used to guide ships from port to port. Navigation on the high seas was by dead reckoning using hourglasses and compasses, then by progressively more accurate navigational devices such as astrolabes, quadrants, octants, sextants then radio signals and finally GPS. Long before GPS, mapmakers used reports of early explorers to draw previously unknown coastlines to scale. Those maps led to still greater and greater discoveries. Cartography was and remains an art although the use of maps is rapidly being replaced by handheld Global Positioning devices that track location with signals from a worldwide array of satellites orbiting in geostationary positions.

Dr. Lee Spence reviewing shipwreck locations.

Dr. Edward Lee Spence is a marine archaeologist and modern pioneer of underwater exploration. He has a lifetime fascination with maps and, as he tells it, "I read Treasure Island and was fascinated by its tale of pirates and buried treasure. I started burying coins for others to find, imagining the thrill it would give the finders. As I got older I started drawing maps that could be used by others to find some of my small caches of treasure. What I was doing then was similar to the modern Geocaching games of today."

Dr. Spence's propensity for hiding coins continues to this day. Since he is one of the world's most famous shipwreck hunters and an acclaimed marine archaeologist, his zest for finding is coupled with his legacy of leaving coins and artifacts behind for future generations.

"When we break a cup or plate, we don't throw it out. We bury the pieces outside. Someday someone is going to dig them up. Not long ago I went looking for a jar of silver coins that I buried in the dirt floor of our family carport when I was a child and we were living in Georgia. It was money saved from my paper route. I still had the map I had drawn showing where I buried those coins, but I still couldn't find them. The house was gone, the carport was gone. All of the locators or 'signposts' I had recorded on my 'treasure map' were long gone. Perhaps if my map is ever matched up with an old plat of the property, my 'treasure' could still be located."

While Lee's paper route money disappeared with the landscape, that was not the case with silver dimes and quarters he secreted under the corner of his family's home on Sullivan's Island, South Carolina when he was a teenager. Decades later he took his son Matthew, to look for them. Using a metal detector Matthew, then just ten years old, quickly found Lee's buried trove of coins. It was a youthful legacy Lee found both fun and rewarding to share with his son.

Times have changed since Lee was a kid. "I could buy antique maps for twenty-five cents. That was half my weekly allowance," he proclaimed from his treasure filled offices outside Columbia, South Carolina. A bank building with a three-foot thick vault door served as his repository for many of the shipwreck coins and valuable artifacts Lee has discovered under the oceans of the world. He still buys antique maps but has paid thousands for them.

"While I was in college I went to the National Archives. I found out that the Government Printing Office was still selling nineteenth-century maps for their original issue price, as long as they still had them in their inventory. That might be fifty cents or a dollar. I bought many navigational charts from the 1800s. The most expensive one was $2.50."

Lee pursued mapmaking studies and eventually a lucrative career finding shipwrecks and making shipwreck maps and charts. "When I went to college there were no programs in underwater archaeology. So, because I figured I would need mapping skills, I started out in Civil Engineering. I later took a number of cartography courses including one in interpretation of aerial photography and another in computer mapping." Lee won the Donald O. Bushman Cartography Award from the University of South Carolina's Cartography Department.

Of course, not all of Lee's early map making was the romantic stuff like plotting positions of sunken galleons or pirate ships laden with booty. Lee worked for the engineering firms of Davis & Floyd then G.W. George in Charleston. Officially he was a draftsman, but he had worked on a survey crew and in his heart, he was a mapmaker. "I drew all sorts of site plans and maps. Davis & Floyd is now a major firm, but at that time I was the only real cartographer they had. My favorite was making topographical maps or topos. I could do every aspect of a topo survey, from pulling chain to turning angles and running levels, from reducing the field notes to drawing the finished plat. A lot of what I did was laying out new streets, lots and sewers for developments."

Undaunted by the routine, Lee avers, "I love drawing maps. A lot goes into it. How you draw a map greatly affects people's perception. On a flat map of North of America, Greenland is gigantic in comparison to the way the same island appears on a globe. Depending on who is drawing a map, it might be used to twist realities and affect political or other goals. In the old days maps were used to convince people to explore and settle the interior of our country. Look at a highway map versus a map made for commercial interests; they can be vastly different. A town's name can be in big or small lettering depending on who is paying for the map and where they want to direct your attention and your tourist dollars."

"I was fascinated by *National Geographic Magazine*'s shipwreck charts. Some showed shipwrecks. Some of my maps show you how to get to specific shipwrecks that I have already found, while others are based largely on the historical records of shipwrecks rather than fieldwork. Some deal with a special period like the Civil War. Others cover hundreds of wrecks spanning hundreds of years. Maps I draw for publication are usually decorative and meant for people to hang on a wall."

One of Lee's most popular maps has sold over 30,000 copies. It is a chart of Civil War shipwrecks in the vicinity of Charleston. "For each wreck on my map, *Shipwrecks of the Civil War*, I used a small, very simple sketch showing the type of ship to represent its location. The pictured wrecks included ironclads, steamers and sailing vessels, and in most cases I showed their rig so you could differentiate between a schooner and sloop. The wreck of the Mary Bowers sits on top of the *Georgiana*. But a sketch of that would have been confusing. Instead, I showed the *Georgiana* and Mary Bowers next to each other. Those are some of the individuality and choices a cartographer puts into his work."

Lee has authored many books as well as his seafaring charts based on his meticulous research. "People buying my Civil War shipwreck maps are not just buying my art. Most of them like my maps for the history they portray. The inclusion of shipwrecks, with their lure of sunken treasure, is usually a large part of their appeal. I enjoy making maps as, like my books, they allow me to share my knowledge. But the best part is they are lot faster and cheaper than a book to produce."

Some of Lee's most extraordinary maps are those that he hand colors using techniques map makers of old originated before color printing. "I use watercolors in the antique style. I sell those as limited editions." Lee showed me two early charts that had been hand colored to compare to his work on a Civil War shipwreck map. One map was dated 1758, the other 1790.

"Dealers will buy an atlas, tear out the maps and sell them by the page. This was torn from Guthrie's Geography of 1790, improved by Thomas Kitchen. I purchased it last year for almost $200. I wish I had the whole atlas."

Lee describes his maps as a "natural byproduct" of the painstaking research he has done to locate sunken ships and their treasures. That research requires many years to compile and would never be done just for a chart.

When researching Spanish galleons wrecked in 1715 along Florida's coast in a hurricane, Lee took 240 years old eyewitness accounts left by survivors and salvors and plotted the locations they described on a modern chart.

"Distances from St. Augustine, Cape Canaveral and other known points of the Florida coast were usually given in leagues or miles. But such units of measurement were defined differently in different countries and even the same country changed their definitions over the years. So, according to the nationality of each eyewitness, I converted the distances to modern measurements before plotting them. I plotted and compared all the different descriptions. In some cases, the plotted locations matched up exactly with the location of a shipwreck already known to the company I was working with, in other cases they didn't. But I suspected those wrecks simply hadn't yet been found because in each case the plotted positions were in areas of deep sand. Overall, I was surprised by the accuracy of the early accounts, especially with respect to latitude. My plots confirmed my already held belief that one could use such accounts to find the since lost locations of valuable wrecks."

"Figuring latitude has always been fairly simple. The angle of the earth to the sun changes throughout the year. But, as long as you properly consider the daily change of that angle, which can be done mathematically or by table, you can determine latitude to the nearest degree using noon sun sights taken with just a folded piece of paper. Longitude is far more difficult."

He found many discrepancies between old navigational charts from colonial periods. Most of the differences were in longitude.

"In centuries gone by, each country used a different city to run their zero-degree line of longitude through. That line was known as the Prime Meridian and its placement affected how all other lines of longitude were numbered. For instance, France ran their prime meridian through Paris, while England used Greenwich, which has since become the World Standard. Therefore, longitude on early French maps varies from that shown on those of England, Holland, and other countries. Further complicating it is that longitude can only be accurately determined with an extremely accurate knowledge of both local sun time and clock time at the prime meridian and calculating the difference. Because the world makes a complete revolution every 24 hours, that difference can be used to calculate the longitude. But an accurate maintenance of clock time for the prime meridian was not possible until after the invention of the chronometer in the 1700s."

Early navigation depended on maps made by the first explorers and their sailing masters. "Even the best maps made for the government thirty years ago are often wrong. They are typically off by hundreds of feet; in most cases those errors are really time keeping errors that resulted in longitude errors. Today with GPS we have precise positioning."

Lee's charts of Shipwrecks of Hilton Head and Vicinity, Shipwrecks of Wreck Valley: New York and New Jersey, his majestically framed charts that include bits of artifacts he has recovered from specific shipwrecks are not only collector's pieces but coveted by museums.

Lee's 1995 book, *Treasures of the Confederate Coast: The Real Rhett Butler & Other Revelations,* explained how his research revealed that the Rhett Butler character in *Gone with the Wind* was largely based on a real person. That was an amazing literary discovery because Margaret Mitchell had always claimed her book was pure fiction. Lee's evidence was overwhelming. His discovery made international news.

The real Rhett was a tall, handsome, shipping magnate named George Trenholm from Charleston, South Carolina, who was much admired for his business acumen and his personal bravery. Trenholm's Civil War-shipping efforts earned today's equivalent of over two billion dollars in gold in less than five years. It made Trenholm the most successful blockade runner and the richest man in the South.

Lee recognized the Trenholm-*Gone with the Wind* connection only after researching and finding the wrecks of several Trenholm-owned steamers that had been lost while trying to run through the Union blockade fleet off Charleston Harbor. Lee discovered and explored the rich wreck of Trenholm's finest steamer, the *Georgiana*, and has written extensively about his discoveries on that ship. Some of his map-illustrated certificates of authenticity include a straight pin or glass button that Lee salvaged from the wreckage. Lee also discovered the Trenholm-owned *Delia Maria*, which sank off Hilton Head before the Civil War.

Lee was the first person to discover the Confederate submarine *H. L. Hunley*. The little submarine attacked the U.S. steam sloop of war *Housatonic* and sank it on February 17, 1864. The *Hunley* and its entire crew of nine men disappeared without a trace, until Lee found the wreck 106 years later. The *Hunley* was the first submarine to sink an enemy ship in the history of the entire world.

Government archaeologists were originally content to leave her where she lay but have since described it as the most important underwater archaeological discovery of the twentieth century. The day Lee found the wreck, it was almost entirely buried. He could still view a narrow portion of her upper hull. Fortunately, it was enough to identify it. Lee went swimming to the surface literally screaming underwater "I have found the *Hunley*, I have found the *Hunley*." The seafloor in that part of the Atlantic Ocean is like a vast underwater desert with constantly shifting dunes. The sands reburied the wreck within days.

Lee carefully plotted the location of his discovery and shared his maps with various government officials while seeking permission to dig her up and raise her. He eventually filed an admiralty lien on the *Hunley* in U.S. District Court, claiming ownership based on both the Law of Salvage and the Law of Finds. In 1995, at the official request of the South Carolina Hunley Commission, Lee donated his rights to the *Hunley* to the State. The entire wreck was eventually excavated and raised in 2000. The crew were removed and buried with military honors. The submarine is now undergoing study and conservation at a specially built lab in Charleston. It will eventually be placed in a museum for permanent display.

A map, which Lee published well before anyone else had gone to the site, is proof of his discovery. His "X" is at the exact position where the *Hunley* was eventually raised. "Just like on the old pirate maps, I used an 'X' to mark my spot and sent copies to the government and even included it in my 1995 book," Lee said.

"Once I published its location, anyone who could read a map could go out and dig up the *Hunley*. That was one reason why I was so anxious that the *Hunley* be raised and properly preserved before it was destroyed by souvenir hunters," he explained, looking at his original, hand-annotated chart. He also showed several scale maps that he had sent to various government agencies. Each proves his discovery. In 1976, based on Lee's mapped location, the *Hunley* was nominated by the National Park Service to be placed on the National Register for Historic Places and was placed on the Registry in 1978. A wreck is only eligible for registry if its actual location is known.

Unrolling a print of a hand drawn 1865 chart, Lee said: "One of the best ways to find a shipwreck is to have a contemporary map. The original of this chart was on linen. It was made immediately after the Civil War to map the depth changes in the approaches to Charleston Harbor caused by both intentional and accidental shipwrecks during the war. The location of the *Housatonic* is shown by this wreck symbol and is actually marked by name. The wreck shown over here is unnamed, but it is right where I found the *Georgiana*. I found the original of this chart in a government office in an active file and had this copy made. I found it long after I found both the *Georgiana* and the *Housatonic* so it didn't help me with either discovery. But I was able to use it to confirm the *Housatonic*'s location and to find other wrecks shown on the chart. Some of the wrecks still stuck out of the water when this chart was made, and they were used as benchmarks for turning angles. Over 40,000 soundings with a lead line were made during the survey." Lee explained about the depths shown on the detailed map.

Named for General Robert E. Lee, a distant relative, Lee has family roots as far back as American history can be traced. Dr. E. Lee Spence is a southern gentleman who has become a legend in his own time. A Renaissance man, with discoveries in both archaeology and American literature, whose books and artistry with maps has preserved history for all time.

BOB MARX, TREASUREMAN

"I'm sick so no pictures," Bob Marx growled. He stayed overnight at a friend's home in Tequesta, Florida, forgot his sleeping pills so couldn't sleep.

"He drank Vodka all night," David Foster laughed. David produced a T-shirt that he slung over his friend that had a happy puppy cartoon on it then snapped his picture with a small digital camera. Marx tolerated it then tolerated me as I snapped a couple of photos of him as well. His eyes were swollen and mostly closed, his voice rattled in his throat and when he talked, made the sound of gravel rumbling in a wave, and, for all intents and purposes he looked grouchy.

Bob is a large man, a burly ex-marine, adventurer, and diver. He has explored the world's oceans looking for sunken treasure and has found more than his share. He's also garnered his share of trouble. Big trouble. He excavated the lost city of Port Royal in Jamaica. The English settlement was submerged in the sea after an earthquake and tidal wave struck in 1692. He worked on Port Royal bringing up artifacts and treasure, conserving what was found for more than three years. Marx could not get the Jamaican government to let him continue. He found the legendary Spanish treasure galleon *Maravillas* in Bahamas' waters. He worked well, for a time, with authorities in that country then had a major confrontation. What he called the country's leaders is unpublishable. He still calls them what he called them then and without compunction. Bob was one person that was never politically correct. Like some stand-up comics of our era, he thrives on being politically incorrect and likes to shock audiences with rough talk and raucous stories.

"I knew Bob Marx when he was a nineteen-year-old Marine at Camp LeJeune," Bob Weller related. "Bob has a knack for making enemies," he laughed.

For all of his rough edges, and he had plenty, Bob was in demand as a lecturer. He spoke at the Jupiter Beach Resort to raise money for the museum run by the historical society and regularly lectures on cruise ships like the QE II.

Maybe the rough edges are the result of his education. "I went to first, third and sixth grade," Marx grumbled. "I don't give a HYPERLINK mailto:#@&x #@&x if people know I was in reform school." The tough edge was an act of sorts.

This rough and tumble adventurer had a brilliant mind. He has written more than sixty books, some 800 research papers and articles, and taught himself to read complicated old Spanish in the Archives of the Indies of Seville. He did much of his own principal research into maritime history, received a knighthood from the Spanish queen and said, "I turned down seven honorary PhDs including one from MIT which Dr. Edgerton got me. That one I regretted since it was Dr. Edgerton that got it for me. Edgerton was with me in Brazil, France, Spain, Mauritius, Florida, Mexico, Bahamas. . . ."

As he got into his recollections, Marx softened. His life spanned many generations of great explorers that helped him along the way, shared their inventions and expertise, and took the young diver under their wings as he pursued his great adventure, that continued until his death on July 4, 2019, at the age of 82.

He was born in Pittsburgh, Pennsylvania on December 8. "I'm not going to give my age," Marx growled. "It's all in books. My resume is 22 pages long. It would be longer but I stopped writing it three years ago."

It is in his books, the copyright page lists his year of birth as 1933. Bob gave his year of birth as 1936. This puts his generation of hard drinking, hard living, and high adventure into the world's great era of ocean exploration. Discoveries were being made for the first time. Scuba, self-contained underwater breathing apparatus, was not invented for another ten years and by that time Bob Marx had run away from home and was already diving and getting in trouble.

"Ask and ye shall receive," he said, sipping another cup of Chris Foster's brewed coffee. He sat at their breakfast nook table in the kitchen of a spacious home decorated with shipwreck finds, rare books, and nautical antiques. "It's all in books." Bob Marx was interviewed by television reporters, journalists, and media moguls. He'd been in reform school and jail and relished his tales of woe begone before.

"I don't ask questions," I told him. We worked for the same editor at the late and lamented *Argosy Magazine* long ago so I felt comfortable with the big guy's grouchy demeanor.

"Couple of years ago my grandkids went to Disney. They brought me a T-shirt with 'grouchy' on it. I wore it the day I had three doctor appointments. I told the nurses, 'You got ten minutes to get me in to see the doctor. Otherwise #@$% you and I'm out of here.'"

About wanting me to ask him questions he said, "Everyone else does." Marx said it calmly, smoothing out, relaxing into the spirit of his life of adventure.

"Talk," I told him. Talk he did and he began with something of a quote that is the touchstone of his life, "The best is the next adventure and more adventure." Then, "I have gout. Last night was the first drink I had in four months. It's all in books. How I made my first helmet. How I started diving. How Harry Reisberg inspired me. I'll take that for one of my grandkids." Marx grabbed one of my books off the table that I'd brought for David Foster's son Will. Foster already had copies and when he said so Marx grabbed it. He was always grabbing Foster's stuff including his sun glasses.

"When they're only a twelve-dollar pair I let him. I don't let him steal my sixty dollars sunglasses," David said. His Nashville accent still pronounced even after living the last twenty years in Florida.

"I'll take it for my grandkids. Right now, they're on a flight to California with my wife to visit their 99-year-old grandmother." Her longevity stunned Bob Marx who, at 75, was struggling with his own mortality suffering with heart disease and gout. He's had to have a pacemaker replaced.

I don't see him that often anymore since I've taken myself off the film festival and lecture circuit to research and write my own books. I took it for granted that he'd be around forever. Indestructible, indefatigable, irrepressible, irresponsible Bob Marx. And he had a dirty mouth. He spouted expletives in any company that are not fit to print. He relished the effect he had on people and was old enough not to care if their reaction was negative. He was not opposed to blowing his own horn but was not a braggart. He could denounce himself and, because of his age and imprecations, was a welcome subject for friendly jest and good humor.

"I started to run away from home by age seven. I pedaled a bike all the way from Pittsburgh to Chicago where I got in trouble stealing candy from a blind person selling papers and candy in the Federal Building. I spent a lot of time either running away or in reform school," Marx said.

"At age ten I went to reform school for the next three years in Harrisburg, Pennsylvania. I escaped. Steve McQueen would have been proud of me. I slid down a laundry chute four flights and landed in a laundry truck. I went to Atlantic City." Of this great escape Marx was justly proud.

"I looked in the Yellow Pages under diving and found Joe Novak. He had an old-fashioned rig that pumped air down into a helmet. He'd sing Polish songs. After a while Novak said, 'Why should I do this. You do the diving,'" Marx related.

"I was thirteen. Six days a week I worked with this Pollock. I made a mistake and sent a post card back to Pittsburgh to one of my chums with a return address on it. Cops showed up. Joe picked me up and threw me into the back of his pick-up while his wife, three times bigger than he was, argued with the police. I ended up in Bridgeport, Connecticut, and dove for a company doing contract work which included picking up bodies of test pilots from Sikorsky helicopter. They crashed and I had to pick up parts of the helicopters and parts of bodies."

"I visited Buffalo, New York and dove on an 1830 shipwreck. I brought up Rye whiskey. We got fifty cents a bottle. They sold it for $50 a bottle to night clubs. Shows how divers get screwed," Marx smiled. It was difficult to see the expression change. His face was swollen but his eyes were getting bigger and the thick lids pushed back. His voice and demeanor animated.

Marx stayed with a relative of diver Joe Novak in western New York until he was fifteen. Then California beckoned. "I stayed with an aunt. She had apartments for women. She gave me an apartment in exchange for a job painting and fixing. If you know me, that's a disaster. I put up signs in my ship's engine rooms, 'Keep the captain out.' Anyway, I was a disaster at fixing but I learned about women."

Marx joined the U.S. Marine Corps. It was a milestone in his life. He went to diving school. "I went all over for the Marine Corps. Picking up bodies from crashed planes. We didn't even have tanks. The first tanks we got were triples. They were heavy," he related.

Bob jumped around and went from adventure to adventure without reference to any timeline. He was assigned to the aircraft carrier *Wasp* and went on several Mediterranean cruises. "We showed the flag. They sent sailors and marines ashore in various ports to get laid and spend money. The *Wasp* was an old-World War II carrier. Nobody'd done it before. . . ."

Marx, disinterested in pursuits ashore, began diving in the ports of call where the *Wasp* dropped anchor. "There had been no diving there in the ports. Except sponge and coral divers. Every place I went it was virgin. I'd ask the fishermen where amphorae are. Octopus lived inside amphorae. The fishermen would pull them up, shake the octopus out and throw the amphorae back," he related.

"In 1953 we stopped in the Azores. We had a base there and unloaded supplies. Got thick, thick cables caught in the props. I got the job to cut them off. I looked down and saw a galleon. I dove on it and found my first astrolabe." Bob described this rare early navigational instrument used by Spanish pilots to determine latitude.

"The admiral of the fleet took it and said, 'I'll use it for a paperweight.' I didn't know what it was. I looked at a photo I took of it later and said, I wuz robbed," Marx said.

"We spent five days in Cadiz showing the flag. We were in Moorish country. When we went ashore hoping to get laid, we found the women were being chaperoned. This was in the fifties. Wine was five cents a glass, Scotch sixty cents a bottle. I looked out from the *Wasp* and said, 'If I was a sailor, and say my ass would sink in a storm, where would I go?' I'd look for Abrigo. There were two forts on either side. You could not go near them since they were prisons for Franco's enemies. I got a rubber ducky and tanks. I dove there, the Guardia Civil yelling at me. I gave them. . . ." Here Marx made the universal gesture of contempt recognized worldwide.

"It was the best museum of my life. The whole bottom was paved with statues, amphorae. I loaded up the rubber ducky. Put the stuff on our ship. The admiral and captain had first pick. They took all the heads of the statues. I couldn't take the whole statue up. On the last day I heard the worst noise of my life underwater. The grinding sound of the Sixth Fleet pulling up anchors. I'm six kilometers away in a rubber ducky. They went without Roberto. . . ." Bob paused. He savored the memory briefly.

"I'm in the rubber ducky with my wetsuit. I had nothing else only my dog tags. I had to run into the middle of the thing between the two forts of Cadiz. The Guardia Civil started beating on me. I was saved by two men. They were out riding."

"Don Manuel had been the minister of Culture under the King. He was an enemy of Franco but the Pope made him Papal Nuncio in Spain therefore untouchable. He was a historian. The other man was Don Mauricio, his family owned the largest wine company in Spain, also a historian. I was rescued by two historians. Both went to Eaton University. I'm covered in blood from the beating. One of them got me up on a horse behind him and we rode to their car, a Mercedes. This in an age where there were only tiny cars or motor bikes in the country. This was a real car. We went to the mouth of the Guadalquiver River. I needed stitches. They got me patched up. Those cops really worked me over," Marx related.

His rescuers called the American embassy. "But in those two days I learned more about history . . . it changed my life. They questioned me about what I had seen underwater and I asked them questions. When I got back aboard ship I was put on 'piss and punk.' In the brig five days drinking bread and water. They left without me." Marx didn't really laugh at his own story. He smiled. The lines in his face changed directions and the puffiness, likely from the medication he was taking for his heart condition and gout, moved.

"Then the second Mediterranean cruise. No one ever did it before. It was all virgin," he described diving on virgin ancient shipwrecks, veritable underwater museums.

"In 1954, when I got out of the Marine Corps, I went to Cozumel with Mel Fisher. He had a deal to make movies in sixteen millimeters. Black and white movies for companies like Pan Am and Voit Rubber. There were less than 500 people on the Island of Cozumel. When we finished, I told Mel, 'I'm going to open a hotel.'" Marx described how the people on Cozumel only spoke Maya, not Spanish in those days.

"My first hotel was six poles sticking up. Everybody slept in hammocks. There were no telephones. The first yacht that came in I sent letters to friends in the states. Said, 'If you get to Merida, you can get here to Playa Azul. Today it is the museum in the city. I charged $8 a day including all the food, alcohol and diving. We went into the jungle killing jaguars, manatees. Everything we killed we ate. I stayed on Cozumel four-and-a-half years. I finally had twelve rooms but still slept in hammocks."

"I read articles all the time that proclaim people did all these things in the Caribbean. The first hotel, the first diving vacations. I did it fifty years before. I took people to Tulum. Killed turtles, took turtle eggs. Killed manatees, tasted like pork. People would kill me for that today. I had to eat." Marx closed his story and shifted to his four grandchildren.

"They're actually terrorists, three, five, seven and nine." He began another tale about the bronze cannon that Mel Fisher recovered from the Spanish galleon *Atocha* off Key West. Fisher presented the cannon to the Queen of Spain and it ended up in the basement of the Archives of the Indies in Seville.

"It almost killed me. I had to clean it. I got a couple of gallons of muriatic acid. I was in the basement with the acid fumes. I nearly died."

Chris Foster's father arrived to drive Bob home. He lived in Indialantic near Cape Canaveral with his wife of many years, Jenifer. A lively pit bull ran into the house and wagged what tail it had left.

"I'm allergic to dogs, Bob proclaimed.

"We're taking him," Chris' father, the late Jud Laird, proclaimed just as vehemently.

"Put him in the trunk," Marx growled.

"Put you in the trunk," was the answer.

"How did you get gout?" I asked this veteran treasure diver who survived a wall toppling over on him as he was excavating the lost city of Port Royal in Jamaica and numerous other incidents underwater. He just had heart surgery and was taking heart medication. Gout was a recent malediction. At a party in his honor, the invitation listed some of his close calls. "Bob survived five plane crashes, nine shipwrecks, two shark attacks (one Mako, one Hammerhead) and five times being blown out of the water with explosives." That he survived at all was a miracle.

"I did the Atkins diet. You're supposed to do it for only a few days. I did it for four months. I gave myself gout. It took four months to get rid of it. For Easter my wife made a big lamb and it came back." Whether annals of medical research will support Bob's premise is uncertain, but like most of his stories it made a good tale in the telling.

His feet were in slippers, swollen and discolored. "I can't wear shoes," he grumped as he left the Foster house and said good bye to his gracious hosts.

"I'm going to steal another pair of his sunglasses," Marx said and walked in his fleece lined pantoufles to David's truck, opened the door, and lifted the sunglasses.

"The best is the next adventure. More adventure," Marx said. He was wearing a black shirt emblazoned on the front with the logo of David's commercial diving company, American Underwater Contractors. On the back it read: "Treasure is trouble. The more treasure the more the trouble. Robert Marx, Miami 2003."

I wanted to ask him about his excavation of the treasure galleon *Maravillas* in the Bahamas. "Forget the *Maravillas*. That's another story. I can't get into it. I'm too tired."

"We call him Bobzilla. Don't piss him off," his friend David Foster laughed.

He got into the passenger's seat of a little black sports car. The lively pit bull in the back seat was running back and forth, tongue panting. Marx, wearing Foster's wrap around mirrored sunglasses, still looked cranky. He was off. A remarkable man. Treasureman.

WHAT DO YOU DO WITH THE STUFF YOU FIND

"People are very fed up with plastic. They want real. They want to light their garden. Well brass ship lights were designed to last 25–30 years at sea. It will last another 25–30 years outside," David Culpepper, Sr. said from his warehouse in West Palm Beach, Florida. The place, before David closed his business and transferred maritime artifacts to his son David's salvage business in North Carolina, was a hoot. Nothing had a price tag. It was a trove of nautical items gathered from the far corners of the world. Anything that once was on a ship or used on the seas and oceans could be found among the jumble at Culpepper & Company.

Craig Sevde and his wife Nancy made a four-hour drive from Celebration, Florida, outside of Orlando, to find items for their store. "Our store is called Just Prep. It is all nautical décor but it has to have been at sea," Craig said.

He purchased a large hard-wood spoked ship's wheel for $120. "This is very heavy," he opined as he struggled it to the trunk of his car. "This is our favorite place to come," Nancy said opening their trunk to reveal many other nautical bargains they were lugging home to resell.

A couple from Wellington were returning a shopping cart full of items they rented from Culpepper. They used them to bedeck their winning entry at a Polo Game. "The theme was pirates. We built a ship and a sailboat. We had all the flags from the Caribbean, put sails up. Had a gangplank with a dummy that looked real. The pirate had a rope around his neck," Frank D'Amelio explained.

Frank and his wife Josephine were wheeling a small cannon back inside the fenced yard along with old wooden lobster pot floats, a ship's wheel, and items they'd used to win first prize at the Polo field. "Next month the theme is Hawaiian. We'll be back," Frank called to David Culpepper.

Treasure diver Bill Mathers with a gold chain reproduced in exact detail from one he discovered off the Pacific Island of Saipan on the wreck of a Spanish Manilla galleon.

Diamond-studded gold cross and pendant reproduced from finds Bill Mathers and his dive team made on Spanish Manilla galleon that wrecked off the Pacific Island of Saipan.

David and his son David with their friend David Baker, and a handful of loyal employees, sold nautical antiques and all manner of chimera. Culpepper & Co. was legendary. Items were gathered on trips to remote places around the world. The Culpeppers enjoyed every visitor. David took time to explain the history and provenance of each piece that one day would decorate a home, restaurant, garden, or end up in the prop lot of some Hollywood studio.

Many of the nautical items used by Disney Productions for the motion picture *Pirates of the Caribbean* came from Culpepper's warehouse.

It was a treasure trove of stuff. Some of it rare, some of it old, some fresh from ship breaker's yards, some reproduced in far flung places like the Philippines or China in the same solid brass or glass as the original.

"I was on the north coast of Java. I wanted to buy fishing dugout canoes. Nobody would sell them to me. Outside a village I saw these on a trash pile. I found the owner. He said he was going to burn them. I told him I wanted to buy them to make furniture. They originally thought I was going to use them fishing so wouldn't sell them to me. Dugouts wear out when they drag them over lava rocks," David explained.

The dugouts were cut in half. David had them standing on end with shelves built inside for books or decorative items. Faded colors were left on the wood just as they were found in Java. The canoes were stored outside in Culpepper's yard to continue to mellow until some person discovered just the shelf needed for a special corner.

"The big canoes are used for fishing in the sea. When they wear out we get them and make table tops out of them for restaurants and bars," David explained. The shipment he obtained from his recent trip to Java and Indonesia arrived in containers and had been unpacked. In addition to dugout canoes made into shelves, there were chests and planks and exotic woods everywhere.

Iron wood, teak, mahogany. Thick finished boards of mango and tamarind wood stood against shelves near a huge stuffed polar bear. "This is going out to a restaurant chain," David said. He had to squeeze past the bear to put his hand on a thick teak board. "It's all from my last trip to Java." The wood would grace any bar or offer great conversation if made into a coffee table.

"These are stamped 1893 and 1907. They are ironwood railroad ties. Ironwood is related to lignum vitae. It is so heavy it will sink in water. The government of Java won't allow shipment of just timber. It has to be a finished product. That provides work for the population. So, I had these railroad ties made into table tops," he said.

The unusual dark wood was beautifully finished with a natural patina. Nail holes and in some cases ancient nails were left in place. The ironwood tabletops sold for from between $120–225.

Across an aisle were coat racks made from old boat wood. The odd shapes and patina created original decorative art suited for a practical purpose. "We did a bunch of benches. They all sold except for this one," David said, moving through a portal to gain entrance to the warehouse inside. There was really no place for the eye to come to rest. Every shelf, every aisle, every nook and cranny was piled with stuff.

Antique Japanese hard hat diving helmets, left as David bought them on one of his travels, lined a shelf. The helmets sold out quickly for $1,300 to $1,500 each. Around the corner, behind a wall of ship's lanterns, steering pedestals, hardwood wheels and binnacles, was a case of rare antique ivory sculptures. Next to the glass case were wooden letters and numbers made from old ship's wood. Original color and patina are left in place.

"We sell them three for $20. I'm getting ready to leave in May for China and the western coast of Java," David said. "My son is in India today. He'll go to Bangladesh. There are lots and lots of wrecks off the Java coast," this former golf ball diver said.

Yes, David grew up in Florida and earned money in his youth diving for golf balls in lakes at some of Miami's most fashionable courses.

"I had Jackie Gleason and Arnold Palmer balls." Another story was brewing. "Alligators never were a problem. They swam away if I touched one by accident. It was alligator snapping turtles that were dangerous. They would bite you. They were just vicious. The tail looked like an alligator. One lake had lots of golf balls. I couldn't get a quarter-bag and he'd come at me. He got my fins a couple of times but didn't get me."

"This is a seventeenth-century Fourth Order lens from a lighthouse. It was invented by Louis Fresnel. It was the laser of the time. Put out a narrow beam of light. It was driven by a clock movement. The base floated in mercury so it took very little energy to turn it. I don't know what that is," David said. His discussion about the rare lighthouse lens was interrupted answering a question about a large tamarind wood ball. "Maybe it was used in rice production."

The unknown was easy to find but not always easy to identify. Ship's hardwood wheels were stacked the length of a rear wall. Ship's brass bells, left just as they were discovered in breaking yards around the world, unpolished and original, were on shelves. "They are $18 a pound," David told one customer.

"I'm going to make more furniture," he said. A curio cabinet made from dugout canoe wood held bronze hermit crabs. The bronzes were unique, piled one on top of another. The cabinet was hand crafted with skill; its window wood finished down to natural color. The drawers were left with original faded but ornate colors of dugout canoe wood. The bronze crabs cost $75 to $85 each.

"In that part of the world I buy everything with a dose of salts," David laughed. He was being asked about a bronze pot he brought back from Southeast Asia. "For every rule an expert will espouse there is an exception. I love finding really cool things you can change to use," David reflected.

Decorative art and junk that can be made into home furnishings with the right eye and proper touch. When you feel like decorating your cottage, beach house or mansion on the water, when only the real thing will do, look for nautical antiques or discover your own on shipwrecks.

SHIPWRECK ARTIFACT DÉCOR

He lived on the top floor of a condo overlooking the Atlantic Ocean. The building is named South Quay in Old Port Cove. An open-air balcony and floor to ceiling sliding glass doors offer breathtaking views of marinas and blue water. Among fine porcelains, cut crystal, and antiques is a collection of ship's hardware: large brass binnacles, engine telegraphs, steering columns, fog horns, and running lights.

"I call it industrial art," Claus Fuchs said. Collecting and restoring nautical antiques is his passion, that and riding his motorcycle. For this one-time Washington, DC based Chief of Engineering for Comsat, old brass, bronze, and copper from ships, that have seen service on the high seas and once voyaged around the world, is as alluring as sculpture and art.

Claus could stand in front of his living room window, took hold of the ship's wheel and set a course anywhere his imagination took him. It is an unusual hobby but one that enables him to discover nautical treasures in junkyards and antique shops then turn them into working, polished gems to decorate his home.

Maritime artifact restorer and collector Claus Fuchs with a ship's telegraph he brought back to working condition.

"This was made in Denmark. All the nuts and bolts are made on the English system. The ship had to be made for British offshore oil and gas support. It weighs 350 pounds. It's a hydraulic thing. The pump inside is stainless steel and bronze. I took it apart and polished it inside and out." Claus is meticulous. When he says polished, everything shines. The large ship's steering column and wheel are based on a wood platform. That too shines as do all of the antique teak bases he uses to display and support his collection.

"Most of this comes from Culpepper's Nautical Décor in West Palm Beach. I'd go down there and spend hours. This compass is early 40s. Somebody took it off a British ship and mounted it on this platform," Claus said. He went to a ship's compass that had somewhere and somehow been adapted for use on another vessel, probably based in India.

"This is primitive welding. I think India or Bangladesh. It has been mounted on a copper steam pipe. There are no compensation balls so I assume it was used on a wooden ship where there would be no metal interference with the compass. Otherwise they would have to set the iron compensation balls to make adjustments. It is a good compass that has been given third world application. The wooden base is teak. I worked on it three weeks. It had been hollystoned so much when it was part of a ship's deck that there was hardly anything left of the screws." His work is precise and admirable.

"Every ship gets a maker's plate. They are cast in bronze usually. The plate tells where the ship was built, what year and has a number. This one is from Norway." Claus has fashioned end tables from bronze and brass maker's plates. Glass tops show off the design and make the table useful for glasses or cups. In most cases maritime records reveal the history of the vessel. Claus has corresponded with shipyards to obtain pictures and information about the ship that once bore the maker's plates. Many met their fate in breaker's yards in India, Bangladesh, the Philippines, and China.

One compass and binnacle Claus is restoring, lovingly polishing it with Wendl brass and bronze polish imported from Germany by Reckitt Benckisser, shines in his workshop. "You can see why my wife Elizabeth no longer her walk-in closets has," he laughed. Two large walk-in closets in what would have been a den had been turned into storage for his tools. The den was an office-workshop. "You can't polish brass on a white carpet. I put towels down."

The tell-tale compass has two sides. One that could be seen on the bridge where it was installed at the steering pedestal, the other side seen below deck in the captain's cabin. A series of lenses magnified the underside compass so that the captain, lying in his bunk in his cabin directly below the bridge, had only to look up to check his vessel's course.

"I never saw anything like it. The compass was made by Weems in Bremerhaven, Germany. The brass binnacle was made by Navis-Plath in Bordeaux, France. A combination French-German firm.

Nearby were ship's bridge and engine order telegraphs. Each was carefully restored. Each piece in perfect working order, ship shape, as when used on a World War II era Liberty Ship, long ago sent to a breaker's yard for scrap. There are Liberty Ship hatch covers in pine and teak wood, bronze wrenches from mine sweepers, a bronze air horn from a German tug boat marked Zollner, Kiel. It is called a "Makrofon."

"These apartment doors are bland. I used flooring. This latch is from Culpepper's. The wind blows the door shut so I have this ship's latch to keep it open. This old auto horn is what my guests use. They reach in like so, toot the horn, open the latch and come in."

"I do this for fun. I have many hobbies. I wonder how I could ever have held down a full-time job," this affable collector of nautical decorative items laughed. Visiting his home is like taking an ocean voyage long ago.

"Today's ships have nothing made of wood, bronze or brass. They are steered with little levers on the bridge. Push buttons," David Culpepper said from his warehouse where everywhere there was a jumble of raw material for decorators with a nautical bent.

FOLLOW YOUR DREAMS

"Your Dad used to say, 'Today's the Day.'" Bob "Frogfoot" Weller once told Taffi Fisher Abt. Taffi was making a video of Bob and Margaret's treasure exploits. They enjoyed many shared memories about her legendary father who died of cancer in 1998.

"My credo is 'Follow Your Dreams,'" Bob smiled. A credo he and Margaret realized and shared with a community of treasure divers living the last great adventure.

Commander Robert "Bob Frogfoot" Weller passed over the bar on October 13, 2008. Were he alive today he would encourage you to "follow your dreams!"

INDEX